"You Say WHAT, Lord?"

A JOURNEY INTO TRUST

GWEN BIBBER KIMBALL

**THE STORY OF THE
COMMUNITY CHAPLAIN SERVICE**

You Say What, Lord? by Gwen Bibber Kimball
Copyright © 2010 by Gwen Bibber Kimball
ISBN: 1-59755-243-7
ISBN13: 978-1-59755-243-1

Published by: ADVANTAGE BOOKS™
                www.advbookstore.com

All Rights Reserved - This book and part thereof may not be reproduced in any form, stored in a retrieval system, or transmitted in any form by any means (electronic, mechanical, photocopy, recording or otherwise) without prior written permission of the author, except as provided by United States of America copyright law.

First Printing: March 2010
10 11 12 13 14 15 16   10 9 8 7 6 5 4 3 2 1
Printed in the United States of America

DEDICATION

*To my dear husband, Dave, who regards CCS
as the "apple of his eye," and who would
have done his own writing had he been able.*

Genesis 12:1-6
*And the Lord said to Abraham, "Go forth...to the
land which I will show you...and I will bless you...
and you shall be a blessing....
And Abraham went forth...and pitched his tent....*

Hebrews 11:8-10
*By faith Abraham obeyed...not knowing where
he was going, to a place he was to receive for
an inheritance with his heirs....
for he was looking for a city whose architect and builder is God.*

CONTENTS

Acknowledgments		v
Chapter One	"And You Shall Be a Blessing"	1
Chapter Two	Ur to Eastport	3
Chapter Three	David	6
Chapter Four	The Tent	9
Chapter Five	The Cottage	12
Chapter Six	One-on-One	15
Chapter Seven	The Penthouse	17
Chapter Eight	CCS	19
Chapter Nine	Pick and Shovel	21
Chapter Ten	14 Greenbrier Drive	23
Chapter Eleven	Glenn	25
Chapter Twelve	Decade One	28
Chapter Thirteen	Walt	30
Chapter Fourteen	The Inheritance	33
Chapter Fifteen	Decade Two	35
Chapter Sixteen	Caring and Sharing	39
Chapter Seventeen	Earl	42
Chapter Eighteen	CCS Canada	46
Chapter Nineteen	Chaplains	50
Chapter Twenty	Nana and Grampa	53
Chapter Twenty-one	Overview	57
Epilogue		60
Appendix	Chronology of Dates and Major Events	62
Addendum 1	Our Chaplains United States	64
	CCS Canada	68
Addendum 2		69
About the Author		70

ACKNOWLEDGMENTS

This is the story of the Community Chaplain Service, a story which is a joy to remember and retell to the many who may not know how it all started. It is a testimony to God's persistence in our lives when He desires to use "whom He will," even though we at times are limited by our humanness. It is a testimony to God's sovereignty and His condescension to "will and to do of His good pleasure" through frail human beings.

We wish to thank the many who caused CCS to become a reality: the first three Board members, Walter Peterson, Lou Boscombe, and Etta Currier, all now deceased, who had the courage to pioneer in new territory; the many who were there by their prayers; those who supported us financially in the early days, and the work as it developed; and those who just simply were in our lives as our family, our friends, and our caregivers. Without you there would be no book.

We especially thank our daughters for their willingness to read these pages, to listen and critique repeatedly, and to make suggestions for additions and deletions. It must have had its times of tedium.

My thanks to my brother, Bud, who asked at the onset of my project, "Are you planning to write this story on a tablet with a pencil?" At my age my answer was, "Well, yes, of course," where upon he replied, "Oh no, can't do that. You need a word processor," which became our daughters' family-project Christmas gift to me. After some weeks of frantic and mostly negative effort, losing one chapter three times to somewhere, but with the aid of daughters who were more up-to-date in such matters, I became able to function productively and soon saw the wisdom in progressing from tablet and pencil. Now I can't imagine having done it any other way!

Our thanks to our friend Ted Nichols, who has a degree in journalism, for taking a day of his vacation to apply his proofreading and editing skills to this manuscript.

To all those who added their wise guidance in the light of my total inexperience in journalism, I express my profound gratitude. Reverend W. Glyn Evans of North Kingstown, Rhode Island, provided me with my first glimpse into the real world of publishing and I thank him for his candid encouragement and suggestions; Mr. Leslie Stobbe of the Evangelical Association of New England offered valuable counsel; CCS Director Walt Dryer made office records and copier available, and showed nothing but patience and graciousness with my many phone calls; Associate Pastor Clint Eastman of Mullein Hill Church of Lakeville, Massachusetts, took time from his busy life to read and evaluate the manuscript. To Glenn,

Walt, Earl, and Ruth, my thanks for their contributions to the actual text. And to Mr. Al Whitaker, Chairman of the CCS Board, for his role in making this a reality, we extend our deepest appreciation.

To my friend, Joannie Parent, who got me off "dead-center" by telling me that a wonderful story like this should be written down and not lost, my special thanks. Her comment became the catalyst!

Chapter One
"AND YOU SHALL BE A BLESSING"

Picture Helen sitting in her geri-chair in the corner, hands resting idly in her lap, eyes looking at nothing in particular, waiting for the only bright spot in her day—her next meal.

Helen will be ninety in November. She is a widow and has one son, somewhere. Her home is an elder care center.

She feels cut off from everything that has been normal in her life and she hungers for someone with whom she can converse.

Chaplain Mel found her in her loneliness one day and made himself available to her as a friend and confidant. Helen shared with Chaplain Mel her lack of assurance that she would be in Heaven, her need to know she was forgiven, and her desire to experience peace with God. Mel explained the Navigator Bridge Illustration to her, and she exclaimed, "What a wonderful story!"

Chaplain Mel assured her that this was not just a story, but an illustration of a loving God's provision for HER. With tears in her eyes, as she now understood for the first time the truth about God and herself, she asked for forgiveness and thanked the Lord for His gift of pardon and salvation.

Chaplain Mel, with his warmth and his smiles, became her regular visitor and her tears returned often whenever her chaplain friend reminded her of that freeing and healing prayer.

Not all residents in nursing homes are elderly: some are there because debilitating illnesses have rendered them unable to care for themselves or even to be tended by their own families. Such was the case with Joe, paralyzed from the chest down with multiple sclerosis. He could still feed himself fairly well with his right hand, but his left arm was useless.

As a sergeant in the Army Joe had served in Germany for three years—time spent in womanizing and excessive drinking. Near the end of this service he was hospitalized, but was not diagnosed then as having MS.

Fortunately, because his problems were noted on his papers, he received government financial aid for MS, which was finally diagnosed at the age of forty-five.

By that time he had married, raised a son and daughter, lost his son in an accident, and witnessed troubles in his daughter's life. When Joe was fifty, Chaplain Mel came into his life at the nursing home and found him wondering if he was being punished by God for the wild life he had lived while in the service.

Mel was able to explain God's forgiveness through Christ, that bridges of religion, good works, and morality are good, but not good enough, that only the cross of Christ could take him to a Holy God.

Joe prayed for God's forgiveness and affirmed to the end that his faith was in Jesus Christ. Chaplain Mel stated that he and Joe had great times studying the Scriptures together, and sharing lunch every Thursday at noon. Joe freely told others of his new faith until his Home-going in 1996.

Chaplain Mel, along with nearly forty other chaplains, is there and ready to help meet the needs of these and many other nursing home residents along the East coast and in Canada because of an organization known as Community Chaplain Service, Inc.

As we view the organization, we are filled with a sense of wonder at what God did when He launched such a ministry to this huge portion of our society. He used a normal pastor and his family who only desired to be where God wished them to be and to do what God wished them to do, even though there were times when they literally did not known where they would put their feet when they were already poised for the next necessary step. They were to learn that their knowing was not important because God knew and He was there as He promised He would be.

Such is the intrigue, and joy, of a sadly diminishing practice among Believers, that of just plain trusting God.

With a profound sense of enthusiasm and excitement we share with you the story, complete with its humanness.

Chapter Two
UR TO EASTPORT

It was late spring, 1973.

It was also bedtime. The resources of strength and courage for the day, which God promises His children, had been used up and it was time to draw upon the resource of sleep. These had been days of praying and wondering: just what was ahead? What did God want of us here in northern Minnesota—was our work done and if so, where would be our next "tour of duty"?

We seemed torn between the urging of important human voices in our lives to stay and continue, and yet there was a vague notion that we needed to think beyond those urgings, but that area seemed to be only a vacuum. So we did what we knew to do: searched the Scriptures, prayed earnestly, and tried to be very alert to God's leading.

Recently we had experienced some nights of restlessness and had found reading to be comforting during those times, so in order not to contribute to each other's wakefulness with lights on, Dave retired to the guest room at the other end of the house. I took my Bible to bed and found myself meditating on Genesis 12: "Abraham went out, not knowing where he was going, and dwelt in a tent." After pondering this for a bit I crossed the hall into Michelle's room. Michelle was our newly acquired twenty-two-year-old daughter who made her home with us after a recent illness.

Home in Minnesota was an attractive ranch house on a hillside, fifty stepping-stones above a lovely lake with a small boat dock complete with a canoe owned by our doctor-friend. We swam there in summer with friends and church young people, and found the canoe a source of enjoyment either as we drifted quietly and watched for wildlife on our way to the end of the lake, or as Michelle and I often "dug in" with our paddles to see how fast we could cover the one-mile stretch back home.

In winter the hillside became a toboggan run for our church kids, with toboggan donated by one of our families, styrofoam cups of hot chocolate parked in the snow, and a rope laced between trees to assist in the laborious haul through thigh-deep snow back up the hill.

Soon after our arrival there we had stood on our dock, looked at our snug home on the hill and at the star-studded sky, and said, "This is so lovely. What a shame we don't have someone to share it with." In due time, enter Michelle, needing home and healing, and who by now had been with us a year and who was a cherished member of our family.

As I crossed into her room that night, I shared with her my quiet yet compelling conviction: although the future did seem uncertain, as Abraham was able to trust his God, so could we trust, without fear or concern, and without knowing. As we talked together about his life, his example became both challenging and comforting. And so to sleep.

In the morning I went out to our den where Dave was already enjoying his "wake-up" coffee, and his first questions was, "What's on your mind this morning?" My immediate thought was, "I'm the Indian here, not the Chief, and this could be a very significant subject in our lives, and shouldn't come from me." I felt absolutely compelled not to say a word about Abraham so I turned and looked out the window at the lovely lake behind our house while I gathered my thoughts. As I did so, Dave said, "Let me tell you where the Lord took me last night. It was Hebrews 11." I began to cry, something that is not typical of me. Mystified, Dave asked why I was crying and I replied, "It's okay, continue your story." He proceeded.

He told me about his reading of God's instructions and promises to Abraham, who was to go out by faith, not knowing where. God's promise of an inheritance to Abraham and his heirs totally escaped our attention at the time, but we would be reminded of it later. The instructions were what gripped us both, and I'm sure God meant that to be: we could handle only one major concept at a time! Dave commented on Abraham's trust, that even though he had sparse information for such a move, he obeyed.

I then recounted my Genesis 12 experience, at which point Dave not only understood my tears but was electrified at the obvious hand of God: two people, opposite ends of the house, opposite ends of the Scriptures, same message! What did it all mean?

We shared our dilemma with our other girls, Midge, who lived in Michigan, and Karen, who lived in Minneapolis, as we tried to make sense out of this totally mystifying development.

The following days were filled with much discussion and prayer. "Lord, what are you saying to us? Are you really and truly saying anything to us?

But how could this be just a coincidence, Lord? And we know You don't play games like this with your children, but this is scary, Lord!"

How good our Father is to permit us our fears and questions, and at the same time go right on with His plans for us: Lord, we do mean it when we say, "What time I am afraid I will trust in Thee." (Psalm 56:3)

Finally, although somewhat disbelieving that we were doing it, we completed plans to resign and move. "What direction, Lord?" God seemed to point us "back east," not surprising, perhaps, because that was home to all of us, Dave and Michelle both having come from Massachusetts, and I from Maine.

On the coast in distant southeastern Maine in the town of Eastport, my hometown, we owned five lovely acres overlooking Passamaquoddy Bay. No house, just land.

"But what do we live in, Lord?"

Oh yes, Abraham in a tent.

"Our pop-up, Lord?" "As you say, Lord. Another church, Lord?"

Probably (our idea!).

So, we packed clothes and the necessities for living for several months at the most, perhaps. Everything else we owned? Into storage.

Chapter Three
DAVID

In order that you might better know the man whom God is desiring to lead on an unknown path, we must go back some years. Picture a small boy, a shock of straight sandy hair, a big mischievous grin, high-top boots. Add a collie dog, and you have a mental image of Dave Kimball, age five.

Born in Mansfield, Massachusetts, the younger of two sons belonging to Otis and Grace Kimball, Dave remembers living in many locations, with his brother, Robert. Chiefly, though, he remembers Waldoboro, Maine, where his father farmed and the boys attended school, helped with the chores, tramped hay, etc., and in winter did their most favorite thing, coasted on their sleds down the long hill which sloped to the river; and later on in Franklin, Massachusetts, doing many of the things done by growing boys which identified him as just that: a growing boy. His scholastic ability hardly had a chance to present itself during those years of having such fun just barely staying out of trouble!

Farmer Foster came to the church one winter (he farmed summers and held revival meetings winters) and this year he spent one week in Franklin. The family attended and Dave heard that all men need a Saviour. He decided that the message included eight-year-old boys, so the small boy made a decision that night which became the foundation for the life of the man.

Life went on as is normal for boys: learning to swim in Beaver Pond; poling around on a rickety raft even when the water was really too cold to risk falling overboard; hiding under the back porch with friend Tommie to try out a cigar belonging to Tommie's father and being found by Dad K., thereupon hearing the pronouncement of the dismal future awaiting boys who stole, sneaked, and smoked cigars.

Many moves followed over the years, as his father managed a multitude of grocery stores, going from one to another to improve their general quality. During those years, Dave was a typical youth—among other things he was a Benny Goodman Big Band fan. A huge decision presented itself to teen-David one night—attend an A&P employees' meeting (he was doing part-time work for his dad) or go to Boston's Metropolitan Theater and hear the famous Mr. Goodman and his musicians, live! No contest. The concert was a huge success, and besides, who would even miss just one more part-time worker? Dad would, but for some strange reason, David has no memory of his father's reaction to his decision-making capabilities.

His functions at the store included bagging potatoes—fifteen pounds to the peck, which moved along with no problem until one day there was a change of produce—to spinach. Picture the pile of spinach amassed as he resolutely attempted to weigh up enough bags to total fifteen pounds, until Dad appeared and suggested with a wry smile that for spinach he might try three pounds to the peck! But, after all, what do teenagers know about potatoes and spinach? He also learned from practical experience the store-wide results of dropping a ten pound wooden box of black pepper on a breezy day with doors and windows open.

His attention to things spiritual during these years was minimal, and his understanding of his faith beyond the very basics remained elementary. His attendance at church and Sunday school were routine and non-productive.

But God had planned a catalyst in Dave's life. Dave had regretted not having a sister, but a close second was his cousin Frannie; during growing-up years whenever the families visited, Dave and Frannie always managed to spend time together "while the old folks talked." Her influence as a committed Christian became significant. After returning from an exhilarating first year at Providence Bible Institute (PBI) of Rhode Island, she pressed Dave with the importance of deciding what he was to do with his life and she urged him to pursue some basic Christian training. The following fall he entered PBI, where he earned his way with such campus scholarship duties as cleaning dormitories, and as a parking valet to satisfy the every-present demands of Mrs. Holmes in the Finance Office. He began to show his real academic potential, and, for the first time, his spiritual life became vital.

Before him lay days of exciting learning, Dr. Ferrin's class in Romans being the ultimate. Dave's grasp of doctrine would be one of his strongest capabilities as he later became a committed "teaching" pastor.

His natural bent for things musical led him into Earle Hulin's Caroller Choir and to the Mountain Top Hour Male Quartet of the great "Ferrin and Booth" days, and it was his privilege to do radio work and to travel with them for several summers as they carried on their evangelistic campaigns across New England.

Marriage to fellow student Gwen Bibber followed his graduation, and attendance at Gordon College, from which he graduated as co-valedictorian of the class of 1946, led to the beginning of thirty years of Pastoral Ministry. Our service was divided among several churches and terminated in Minnesota where our story, like a toddler, took its first faltering step.

God delights in taking ordinary people, from ordinary backgrounds, and doing extraordinary things through them—such is the story of His taking and using David Kimball. The journey begins....

Chapter Four
THE TENT

Our caravan consisted of our car and trailer; our cocker spaniel, Heidi, Karen's VW, bicycle on the rack; and Michelle, Dave, and me with emotions hovering somewhere between excitement and fright.

Some 2000 miles later, we arrived in Maine, in June, at the site of our five acres. Ten years earlier, God had put this lovely land into our lives by a minor miracle. Little had we realized then that these acres would one day become a three-month haven for us in a very unusual time of our lives. The time spent there by the sea was a balm to our spirits in spite of the constantly recurring themes, "Why are we here, Lord?" and at times, "This is crazy, Lord!"

Our first step was to set up our "compound." This consisted of a six-by-nine canvas pop-up trailer with sleeping and limited clothing space for three, and a nine-by-twelve zip-on screen room, complete with plastic storm curtains. We spent our rainy days here, cooking on a two-burner propane stove with fold-up oven, eating at a table with stools, and relaxing in lawn chairs. We locked our groceries inside the aluminum trailer, away from curious little creatures. But when the sun shone we rolled up the storm flaps and moved outside for everything but sleeping.

Along the Maine coast the prevailing southwest wind sets in almost every day shortly after noon. We felt its effects at our campsite and responded by moving our chairs into more secluded spots, and lowering some storm flaps against the breeze when necessary. This southwest wind was responsible for the term "down east." Vessels sailing in a northeasterly direction, "down-wind" before the SW wind, were said to be sailing "down-east"; thus developed the little-understood nickname for this area.

Only occasionally did an offshore breeze produce a day too warm to enjoy the sun. Eastport is affectionately called "the air-conditioned city" due to the cold waters of the ocean which surround Moose Island on which it was built. Summer water temperatures top out at 53.5—not exactly a hot tub! Temperatures on land rarely exceed 90.

The Gulf of Maine is a fog producer—the warm Gulf Stream vs. the cold Fundy waters—so we did have occasions when the whole out-of-doors literally dripped with moisture.

But for the majority of the time we were able to enjoy being outside while we relaxed in a gorgeous setting and waited for God's plan for us to be revealed. We had a minimum of expense—no rent, no phone, no electricity, no utility bills, and of course, no paycheck! We carried our water from a nearby spring, collected wood for the outdoor fire from our own woodlands, and set up our porta-potty cabana, fondly dubbed "Aunt Jane," in a secluded glen of fir trees. When Karen joined us for her vacation we set up our "annex" nearby—an eight-by-ten tent, providing the girls with their own dormitory and all of us with some extra storage space.

Michelle remembers these days as some of the most special of her lifetime. She and Dave had a fun project which eventually became very meaningful to us. They cut a small straight tree of an appropriate size for a flag-pole, limbed it up, peeled it, bought hardware and cord for it, and set it up in the ground on a high spot. That flag flew in the breezes every good day and seemed to be a symbol that this was, for now, our space.

Heidi took on the aura of *born free* as she romped through the woods and open places with ears flying, stopping now and then to daintily nibble wild raspberries from the vines.

We cooked meals over the open fire, picked our own blueberries, raspberries, and mountain cranberries, caught mackerel off the ledges bounding our headland, and occasionally entertained guests for dinner.

We spent time with many old friends, and with my former pastor, Cedric Brooks, and his wife, Verna, who had led me to Christ as a teenager. I remember going to the parsonage with a group of friends after school with half a sandwich saved from lunch. We would sit on the floor around the dining room where we would finish our sandwiches and be fed punch and cookies—sacrificially, I am sure. After all, this was the late thirties in a small Maine town, not exactly an affluent time or place. The main thrust of our being there was lots of conversation: all our big important problems, how Christians handled life, what was appropriate behavior, etc. These interludes were invaluable and helped many of us stay on track. We owed the Brookses a great debt of gratitude.

There was an elevated area of land adjacent to our compound which we dubbed an old sailboat term, the "poop-deck," around which surged the great 28 to 30 foot tides at the mouth of the Bay of Fundy, bringing an assortment of boats, seagulls, fog, and the aromas and sounds of the sea.

These all provided a setting which encouraged meditation, prayer, and, of course, a continual searching for God's plan. Dave spent many hours there in the sun and cool breezes, wrestling with what in the world was going on in his life! After all, when one hits his fifties are not things supposed to be somewhat normal and comfy?

"How old were you, Abraham, when you did all this—seventy-five? That means I should be about thirty-five, according to present-day life expectancy, and I'm fifty-eight! Abraham, were you just a little puzzled, too? I hope so!"

Contacts for other pastorates appeared and disappeared and by September first we sensed the need to be closer to the main-stream in a slightly warmer climate. "Where now, Lord?...New Bedford, Lord? Why New Bedford, Lord?"

Why New Bedford... New Bedford had been home in many ways since our pastorate there at Elim Baptist Church during the Sixties. The church family had been truly a family to us and we loved being in a seaport town. It was nearer to our relatives and seemed a good center for whatever was ahead—contacts for pastorates or whatever it was God had for Dave to do. It was good for Michelle, who had recovered sufficiently to consider returning to nursing, and St. Luke's Hospital in New Bedford was no stranger to her, she having trained and worked there. Beyond those reasons we can only say we felt it was the place for us at the time, so we reluctantly broke camp, said our good-byes to people and land, took in our flag, and took our next step.

Chapter Five
THE COTTAGE

When we neared the New Bedford area on the hot Saturday evening of Labor Day weekend, our immediate destination was a campsite in Bourne Scenic Park, overlooking the Cape Cod Canal. We made camp and readied ourselves with great anticipation for the Elim church service the next morning. The first of a succession of people I shall take the liberty of calling *special angels* (not to be confused with Biblical angels) entered our lives that morning: old friends, Phil and Emma Griffin. They offered the roomy and tree-shaded yard of their cottage by the ocean as a temporary home for our camper and us. They were the first in a series of helpers God gave us to point the way during the upcoming months.

Nearly every day for weeks we commented, "Another day with the Kimballs' name on it": warm sun, moderate temperatures, and little rain—necessities for canvas dwellers. We took advantage of our lovely location while the weather was warm and we swam, enjoyed the yard with picnics galore, had great reunions with old friends, and of course went quahogging (pronounced "ko-hogging") with the Griffins. Phil was an ardent quahogger and made a mean chowder from the hard-shelled sea clams we dug along the shore in shallow water.

When night came, we drifted off to sleep while listening to the owls talking to each other from their various houses. Not at all hard to take!

But eventually things got cold and Phil and Emma urged us to go inside the cottage, which we did, thankful for the extra shelter. It was bright and cheery with just enough space for three adults. During the coldest nights we kept a light burning in the pump room so the water wouldn't freeze, and mornings saw the heater on to entice one to wiggle out from a warm bed.

Dave struggled, sorted out his feelings, worried about food, warm clothes, and shelter from snow and such for his family.

"Oh, my Father, You do remember that our coats, gloves, boots, and winter clothes are all in Minnesota? Just checking, Lord. Help my unbelief, Lord. You did say in Philippians 4:19 You'd supply all our needs according to Your riches in Glory by Christ Jesus, didn't You, and you've done that before for us. Thank you for the reminder, Father."

Dear friends who were to us more *special angels* stayed in close touch and supported us financially and emotionally, and pledged their continued prayer support. What a lot we owe them for following what must have been God's directions to them.

Dave did some substitute teaching and preaching. I was able to help out at Elim as organist on a temporary basis (for seven years!), and Michelle was back at the hospital and was a chief contributor to family expenses, but how we managed on the long haul was wholly His miracle. It was a repeat of the loaves and the fishes, borrowed coats, and bargains from the "Y" Thrift Shop. It sounds so ideal to say that we lived through this in total quiet faith, but there were times of unrest, doubts, and frustration in attempting to determine what this was all about and where it was all going.

"Lord, here we are again with strength and courage lasting until bedtime, and needing sleep to replenish grace for another day.

"Seems we've been here before, Lord. Yes, we can see how that worked out before but—this time? Oh yes: 'My God shall supply...' Why do we have to be reminded again and again. Forgive, please, and apply again to our hearts the message of Psalm 61: 'Hear my cry, O God; Give heed to my prayer. From the end of the earth I call to Thee, when my heart is faint; Lead me to the rock that is higher than I. For Thou hast been a refuge for me, a tower of strength against the enemy. Let me dwell in Thy tent forever. Let me take refuge in the shelter of Thy wings.'"

The evil one delights in taking every opportunity to cause us to wear God's garments to His dishonor, and our hearts are contrite toward those who, on occasion, witnessed in us a level of trust not adequate for "children of the King."

Dave's desire to return to a pastorate was always a very present part of each day's prayer and thought, but there were no developments to encourage him. Enter our next *special angel* and old friend, Mary Jane Pollock, who suggested that Dave talk about his concern with the Reverend Arnold Olson, Associate Minister of Park Street Church of Boston. This wise man of God suggested that perhaps God did not have a church in mind for Dave, but another type of service, one that would expand Christian service beyond the traditional Missionary or Minister stereotype. This thought encouraged Dave to consider broadening his horizons in his quest, so his prayers changed from "a pastorate, please, Lord," to "Lord, what do YOU have in mind?"

We conclude that God waits for us to set Him free to do what He wants in our lives! A quote from our pastor, the Reverend Ken Nanfelt at Mullein Hill Church, seems appropriate here:

"God says, 'You pray, and I will answer, but I'll do it my way.'"

Chapter Six
ONE-ON-ONE

The plight of our next *special angels* came to our attention in October. Larry and Barbara Wetzell, dear friends from Elim, were in the midst of Larry's struggle with Alzheimer's. We had spent many happy hours with these wonderful people. Together, we had camped on our five acres in Maine, had gone on deep-sea fishing trips for haddock off Eastport (always very successful back then when there were plenty of fish), and had enjoyed much Swedish coffee with them! Now their camper sat unused in their yard and they coped as best they could with the changes in their lives.

They were finding life in and out of hospitals and nursing homes nearly devoid of spiritual support. Barbara shared her deep hunger resulting from the months of being away from her church family, and from her inability to any longer have any meaningful communication with Larry. A ministry of holding services in nursing facilities became a thought and prayer, and was tried on several occasions but didn't "gel" sufficiently for Dave to pursue, though he was becoming increasingly aware of the great number of folks who were no longer out there in the pews.

So that Barbara could care for Larry in his own home I helped her set up his room as near as possible to a convenient functioning "unit," showed her how to care for a bed-patient, transfer him to his chair, care for his skin, etc., and buy the proper supplies. With the necessary materials at hand to make his care easier and more secure, Barbara was able to leave Larry with sitters for brief periods. Can you imagine how she loved getting to church occasionally, or going on a shopping spree, or visiting with her sisters!

Larry had been a fine baritone soloist (he had been lovingly called the Bev Shea of Elim Baptist Church) but sadly, Larry no longer had the capacity to communicate intelligently, or to even understand the concept of singing.

One Sunday morning, Dave and I went to Larry's home to "be in church with him" and as we joined him in the kitchen of his home with Barbara, there was before him a television church service to which he was paying scant attention. When Fanny Crosby's old hymn, "Blessed Assurance," was announced, Dave and I moved in close to Larry's wheelchair and sang along, with our arms around him and our heads in close to his. *Larry began to sing and he sang every word in his lovely voice!*

> *Blessed Assurance, Jesus is mine!*
> *O what a foretaste of glory divine!*
> *Heir of Salvation, purchase of God,*
> *Born of His Spirit, washed in His blood.*
> *This is my story, this is my song,*
> *Praising my Savior all the day long.*

We were overcome with a variety of emotions as we observed this response and heard his voice once again. We cheered, and hugged him, gratified that something had penetrated his isolation, even for a brief moment. And there emerged out of the mist, even as the landscape appears when the sun burns away the fog, an awareness of the power of, and the need for, a personal ministry—*One on One! A Chaplain ministry where they were—mostly in nursing homes.*

In his heart Dave finally knew. It had been six months.

"But how do we go from here, Lord?"

God would need to continue being the Architect and Builder of this venture, as He had been all along, because it appeared that Dave was to be a pioneer in a brand-new field, without the vaguest notion where to start!

Chapter Seven
THE PENTHOUSE

By now November was disappearing from our view, and to remain in a summer cottage was no longer a sensible option. Enter Harris Pollock, husband of Mary Jane, to join our roster of *special angels*. He offered us his recently deceased mother's apartment free of charge in exchange for cataloging and packing the antiques acquired by his mother over the years. As Harris said, "Mother stopped dealing a while back, but she never did stop collecting!"

It was a third-floor apartment in a good neighborhood; it needed some decorating, which was long overdue but impossible because of the preponderance of interesting and valuable items with which it was literally filled.

It was within walking distance of Michelle's work, and it was inside—snug and warm—with hot and cold running water that we would no longer have to worry about!

We celebrated a joyous and grateful Thanksgiving dinner at the Griffins' cottage with Michelle, Karen, and Dave's dear step-mother, Ida, after which we cleaned up the kitchen, and washed the floor a final time. As we exited the front door a beautiful rose waved us good-bye, mute evidence of the continuous good weather God had lavished upon us for those several months. Our gratitude to the Griffins is profound; what a difference their cottage made in three difficult months of our lives!

Moving consisted of transferring our sparse wardrobes and our cocker spaniel into the apartment on Maple Street which we fondly called our "penthouse," high up by the tree tops in the breezes and the sunshine, and away from the street noises. Packing and cataloging began immediately and it involved an almost endless procession of empty boxes in, boxes packed, and packed boxes out. It was an interesting challenge, and it was fun, and when it was finished weeks later, Harris purchased the materials, we papered and painted, and it was a joy to live there!

Later that winter, I learned of a Private Duty Registry for Nurses at the Hospital. This type of duty was less rigorous than regular floor duty and was something I felt I could handle physically, considering my status as a back patient. I applied, presented my credentials, and, after orientation, was admitted to the Registry. Thus began a source of income that was deposited faithfully in the bank toward a very special account. Somewhere in Minnesota did we not have a houseful of belongings that we had not seen for nearly a year, and that by now had become only distant acquaintances?

By April, 1974, we had enough in that account to make the arrangements for having our possessions start their journey east! What excitement! It was like planning for the return of dear old friends after a year abroad! However, we had a small problem: our present quarters could not possibly accommodate all that would be on that van.

Enter our next *special angel*: Ella Banks Persson, age 70. Ella had been the organist at Elim Church for many years, and was now retired and living in the Pine Hill Acres section in the north end of New Bedford. We had visited Ella on that warm Sunday afternoon of Labor Day weekend when we had returned to the area, and we had found her sitting alone in her yard, looking rather forlorn and lonely. She had recently lost her husband, had no children of her own, and few relatives nearby. She did not drive and was feeling very isolated with no convenient way to get around and care for all her needs. We immediately started providing whatever assistance we could: among other things we did some taxi duty; Ella and I went on many a shopping spree, which she dearly loved; Dave took on the care of her yard; she and I began sharing the organ duties at Elim Church; and she responded by inviting us for many a delicious meal—cooking was one of her hobbies.

When Ella learned of our need for space she immediately offered her new, clean, but now-empty garage for our overflow. Another detail resolved! Again we recognized the specific hand of God in making provision for us on this mission we were increasingly confident He had set before us.

The arrival date was set and excitement ran high! I promised Dave, "When that van comes down the street I plan to cry!" I did stand at the window and watch, and saw it turn the corner, but everything happened at once. The van arrived, friends came with a truck to transport whatever would be going to Ella's and to help unload, the driver handed me a checklist. . . I got so taken up with the activity and excitement I forgot to cry!

By mid-afternoon, we were inundated with cartons, wardrobes, furniture, and joy! Christmas on a grand scale! It was like a great homecoming and seemed to signify the passing and closing of a chapter in our lives.

Chapter Eight
CCS

While we were cataloging and packing, in searching out "How do we go from here, Lord?" Dave chose as his first confidant a much loved and respected friend and businessman, Walter Peterson of Milton, Massachusetts, Chairman of the Board of Eastern Refractories of Lexington, Massachusetts. Following dinner at the home of Walter and his wife Grace one evening, as we sat before the fireplace, Dave related his story and proposal for this new ministry. Walter found the idea of a one-on-one ministry to be absolutely exciting. His confirmation and encouragement helped supply the impetus Dave needed to forge ahead and seek other capable advisors. Dave realized that a work of significance would need careful direction.

Dave eventually asked Walter to be his first Board member, an invitation to which Walter readily agreed with enthusiasm, and the organization, Community Chaplain Service (later known as CCS), was born.

One of the first churches to respond with the need for financial support was, predictably, Elim Baptist Church. Church Treasurer Joe Teser graciously agreed to act as Treasurer pro-tem for CCS, a service he rendered until a functioning Board was in place.

As a three-member Board was chosen, Walter became the first chairman, with the other members being Etta Currier, businesswoman of Plymouth, Massachusetts; and Lewellyn Boscombe, a certified public accountant from Swansea.

Henry Dumas, another certified public accountant, became the first full-time treasurer, and obtained the original tax-exempt status for CCS. He also set up the computerized mailing list which he maintains to the present time, with its now more than five thousand names.

Dave began visiting an ever-widening sea of nursing homes to sound them out on such a ministry. Administrators and activity directors were, for the most part, enthusiastic about the opportunity to have a chaplain who would become well-known to the residents, and who would be relating to them on a regular and personal basis.

As he approached his actual ministry, he readily learned that the prospects were of far greater magnitude than he had dared anticipate, or that he could possibly handle alone, along with the duties of the founding of an organization and promoting its financial base. He had considered an additional industrial and prison emphasis, but pursued this only briefly because of the sheer scope of the nursing home ministry: in 1974, in New Bedford alone, there were thirty nursing homes, with a population of 1,800 residents.

Early on he enlisted volunteers to help him with a variety of personal services to residents, but he functioned as the sole chaplain and was given enthusiastic praise and appreciation from all quarters at the conclusion of his first year.

During that first year, Dave was impressed with the vast number of people in the homes who, as in the churches, had never been touched with the personal presence of Jesus Christ. In many cases, years of church membership had not brought into their lives the knowledge of who Jesus was and why He came, and, of course, there were many who had no background of any kind that would acquaint them with Him. Many others were angry and hurting and did not want a thing to do with any god, much less the One who claimed to care about them. Becoming a friend to them was vital and Dave steadily gained the love and confidence of many who at first were guarded and skeptical.

But supplying free service to the facilities involved would require financing from outside sources. Soon it was obvious that CCS would be a faith ministry, dependent wholly upon what the Board hoped would be a host of challenged individuals and congregations who now would have to be informed of a totally new and worthy missions venture.

Chapter Nine
PICK AND SHOVEL

In his classic methodical manner, Dave immediately started regular reporting to his Board of Directors. Excerpts from his first Annual Report, covering the eight months from May to December 1974, follow:

"The beginnings of the ministry of Community Chaplain Service have their source in both the hidden and obvious leadings of God. His clear directing to surrender the pastoral ministry and learn new lessons of faith; His opening and closing of doors of service; His use of Godly men to give counsel; His guidance in thought and decisions; all these and more gave clear indication, finally, that this direction of ministry was His purpose.

"The ministry of Community Chaplain Service was initiated in a small way on April 13, 1974, and over the past eight months has developed and expanded in a very encouraging manner. The first convert to Christ was seen on May 29, 1974. Because of the type and age of those with whom we work, there have not been great numbers of conversions, but people are being brought to Christ regularly.

"In initiating the work, financial support was developed primarily among concerned individuals. They saw the need and the challenge and made possible the launching of Community Chaplain Service. At that time very little was done in promoting financial support among churches.

"The CCS ministry has progressed to the place where we are providing full-time service for four nursing homes, and part-time plus 'on-call' arrangements for four more. This covers two cities and two towns.

"The process of incorporation has been relatively slow. It was necessary to write our Statement of Faith, Articles of Incorporation, Constitution, and By-Laws. Then it became necessary to seek out the right persons to serve on the Board of Directors and as Incorporators.

"An area of the CCS ministry now being developed rapidly is the use of volunteers. These can minister to people in many ways and in the process find opportunities for Christian witness. Close contact is maintained with these volunteers in order that guidance may be given to their work and that follow-up work will be efficient.

"The current situation in the CCS ministry is both exciting and disturbing. The excitement is found in the almost limitless opportunities for service and witness. The disturbing element is found in the fact that open doors cannot be entered until a funding level is reached which will permit additional personnel in CCS.

"It is obvious that plans for increased funding must be formulated and implemented. The present level fails to meet all the expenses. A temporary arbitrary salary for the Executive Director has been set at $175.00 per week. At times the payment of a full salary is impossible because of other bills that must be paid. To December 4, the average receipts amounted to $172.12 per week.

"Recently, I have been putting work into CCS among churches. I have had thirteen presentations to churches, church boards, and church organizations. These have included six denominational backgrounds. Contacts have been made with nineteen other churches or church groups for presentations in the future—immediate and long-range."

Dave closed out that year with the conviction that he must work persistently to strengthen the financial base to enable the support of more chaplains and meet CCS's future challenges. He entered into this with great resolve, and deputation became one of his major thrusts in 1975. More and more his days were spent in travel and contacts—everyone he knew or ever had known who might be interested, and every reasonable prospect that came to his attention in the process. By the dozens, they were visited personally, with thousands of miles covered by car. A financial base slowly took shape, although small at first, and by the end of the first full year supporters represented ten states and several Church Missions budgets. Records show an average weekly income of $241 for the year 1975.

"Father, this whole idea is yours, and back at the beginning You did promise to supply all needs. We have a long way to go yet—but I rest in my firm knowledge that You know that."

Amen.

Chapter Ten
14 GREENBRIER DRIVE

Life's activities have a way of continuing on—often routinely and doggedly. Dave continued to work on his project, Michelle and I continued to work at the Hospital, Ella continued to talk about the need to move, we continued to joke about "our furniture fills your garage so you can't move," Dave continued to mow Ella's yard, she and I continued to play at Elim, etc., etc., etc....

Then something disrupted the routine and left us blinking! Ella asked, "Why don't you buy my home?"

Now, you can believe that her comment was met with wild hilarity! How could we buy her home? How could we buy anyone's home? We had lived all our married lives in church-owned parsonages: one had been considered the nicest in the state with its four fireplaces and hand-hewn woodwork; another was dreadful, known to us as **the house that Jack built** (of Jack and the Beanstalk fame). The parsonage arrangement was fine in some respects, but it presented a pretty dismal picture when one considered the lack of equity for future private housing. But despite our hilarity at Ella's proposal, it soon became her favorite subject.

One evening as we left Ella's home, Dave said, "I think we should stop joking about buying Ella's house and start praying about it."

My literal response was, "You must be out of your tree!"

I then tiresomely rehearsed our financial situation as if Dave did not already know it, and ended with, "and what would you suggest we use for a down payment?"

Dave met my challenge by very quietly restating, "I think we should pray about it."

I really couldn't think of a good rebuttal to praying, so I agreed—we should pray about it. End of subject, or so I thought.

Shortly after that exchange, it occurred to me that perhaps every possible penny of my paychecks should go into a savings account toward a down payment. I considered this to be a most original and brilliant idea, not realizing that by my willingness to pray about it, God (just perhaps) had given me a glimpse of Dave's vision! Michelle joined the "down payment drive," and life continued, routinely and doggedly.

And as we continued, there emerged an added incentive. Ella's home would provide ample space under one roof not only for the family and all our belongings, but for a home office for Dave's work. Office space was becoming a problem. Dave needed room for desk, typewriter, supplies, files, etc., which we did not have in our third-floor penthouse. That need provided us with a fresh enthusiasm to work and pray toward this goal, and by the fall of 1976, less than two years after Dave's fateful and absurd comment, we had a down payment, and Ella was ready to sell! She not only had found a lovely senior citizen's apartment downtown in a most convenient location, but she was elated that she and Ralph had "chosen our home for us," a comment she repeated with joy many times during the ensuing years.

Moving day in mid-October went smoothly and here we were at 14 Greenbrier Drive—in our very first "own home"! I would not have to stroke our shrubs and flowers good-bye again very soon. I had done enough of that!

Dave's office took shape in the lower level of our new home and he appreciated being able to spread out and work in a roomy environment. We had Ella's blessing in whatever we did to make her former home fit our needs, even though at times it required minor changes, and we saw to it that she spent considerable time with us for meals and special occasions.

What a good God! From a tent, to a cottage, to the penthouse, and finally to this, our lovely modest ranch-style palace, all on God's timetable and all beyond any planning we could have done for ourselves, plus Dave working happily at a Mission to which he was absolutely committed. Who could ask for more? So many of the temporary aspects of the past three years were now at rest. We felt settled and secure in a permanent way, as one feels when one finally arrives home from an extended trip. Does God ever tire of His children giving thanks? I think not!

Chapter Eleven
GLENN

One day as Dave was pursuing his deputation for fund raising and found himself in the Belmont, Massachusetts, area, he stopped to see a young pastor-friend, Glenn Havumaki. Glenn remembers that visit and comments as follows:

"I can remember the day that David visited me at the Evangel Baptist Church, in Belmont. I was serving in my first pastorate after seminary graduation, had been there about a year, and what David shared about CCS and its beginnings grabbed my attention. I had always had an interest in a chaplain ministry, at least since the days right after high school, when I worked at the state hospital in Gardner, Massachusetts, and during my work as an orderly in general hospitals while in college.

"After David left I thought that CCS sounded like a ministry that I might enjoy *sometime*. In fact, I was already beginning to have thoughts that the pastorate was not the place that I was supposed to be, in my service to Christ. Along with my expressed desire toward a chaplaincy, I was also considering that I had a love for small group ministries, suggesting perhaps a position as Minister of Discipling, if such a thing existed.

"I decided to wait until my upcoming wedding was over before making any significant decisions, the reason being that I thought some of these feelings or questions were from general tiredness resulting from pursuing my relationship with Sandy and planning for the wedding. Five weeks after the wedding, I had an experience that I was convinced was of the Lord, and I resigned Evangel, even though I had no place to go. I just knew it was of the Lord and I had a peace about it.

"As I sought the Lord's direction it was still unclear whether I should seek a ministry with CCS or a church ministry that would allow me a staff position in the area of Discipling.

"I don't think I had ever put out a fleece before the Lord before this occasion, nor have I since, but this was a time when I needed God's direction clearly. To minister in CCS meant I had to raise my support and I was not sure I had the faith to believe God would supply. I needed His direction, and I began to lay out fleeces regarding money. He met them all.

"On one occasion I had asked Him to give us $100 between one Sunday and the next. A friend of mine (not a member of the church) had invited us out to dinner after the Wednesday night prayer meeting, and Sandy went to the parsonage to get ready to go out. She had forgotten to take her Bible home with her, and I saw him paging through it, and when we left the Church he said, 'I'll take Sandy's Bible to her.' He knocked at the door, and said to her, 'I like the bookmark you have in a *certain Book*!' She opened the Bible to that spot, and there was what looked like a $100 bill. Dick was a real prankster and she thought that he had probably put a fake bill in that spot that was made to look like the real thing, but with a closer look she realized it was a crisp new $100 bill! God has answered another of my requests to give direction toward CCS.

"I accepted the Board's invitation to become the first CCS chaplain and began to raise funds. Again, God provided in a marvelous way, and by April 1976 I had begun to serve half-time, as I continued to work part-time. By October, I believe, I was full-time with CCS, where I served with Dave until 1979, when I accepted a call to become chaplain of Elim Park Baptist Home, in Cheshire, Connecticut, where I continue to serve to this day.

"CCS was a life changing experience for me, as God changed the direction of my ministry to something I never could have guessed. He provided for us in a wonderful way, one day at a time, as we learned in our early years of marriage to depend upon Him. He not only met our needs but many times our wants, and even gave us the privilege of owning a home at the time that we were the most dependent upon Him.

"He put the right people in the right places at the right times, and constantly reminded us that He was watching over us. This was a blessed experience.

"My years at Elim Park have confirmed the great work that God did in my life during that interlude between a church ministry and an institutional ministry, an interlude that was bridged by CCS.

"My heart was truly blessed as I had opportunity to speak at the Twentieth Anniversary Banquet of CCS, and hear introduced the thirty-two chaplains and associate chaplains who now serve in the United States and Canada. God was beginning the great work of CCS through Dave, and He gave me the privilege of serving as the first chaplain, and of helping Dave see his dream become a reality—that of touching many elderly lives in nursing homes across our nation.

"Surely this growing ministry uniquely touches an unreached-people which comprises nearly 13 percent of our total population."

Glenn was another sign of God's leading not only his life, but Dave's. When Dave stopped to see Glenn he was in no way looking for a chaplain. Rather, Glenn was merely another of those who fell under the heading of *someone he knew* who might be challenged to become a supporter of this service to the elderly. Although prior to this meeting, Glenn had not heard of CCS, he was obviously a person whom God had in place, just waiting for the right time.

Glenn's ministry included many novel innovations and outreach techniques, all directed at a more complete and sensitive service to those under his care, and he was a significant loss to CCS when God saw fit to move him on.

Chapter Twelve
DECADE ONE

A close check on records of the first ten years (1975–1984) reveals these high points aside from events previously mentioned:

- **Selection of the remainder of a full seven member board:**
  Mr. Frank Griffin, Braintree, Massachusetts
  Rev. Dr. David Madeira, Barrington, Rhode Island
  Mrs. Evelyn Ferrin, Barrington, Rhode Island
  Mr. Henry Dumas, Fairhaven, Massachusetts
- **As Board members found it necessary to resign or were deceased, those selected to fill the vacancies were:**
  Mr. William Richardson, Providence, Rhode Island
  Rev. George Buhl, Kingston, Massachusetts
  Mr. David Horton, Marion, Massachusetts
- **Incorporation was pursued for a full year before accomplishment in May of 1975.**
- **Mrs. Ethel Sturgis and Mrs. Mary-Ellen Stroup did part-time secretarial work.**
- **Attendance at Congress (a regional gathering of evangelical ministries involving nationally known personalities) was instituted, with accompanying visual aids and brochures, prepared by layout-specialist Harry L. Bibber (brother of the author) of Alexandria, Virginia.**
- **A vigorous ministry for volunteers was developed.**
- **A greeting card ministry was begun by Glenn and carried on by women of local churches.**
- **Chaplain Walt Dryer came on staff in 1981 and became associate director in 1983.**
- **Continued aggressive deputation was carried on by the director.**

An extensive handwork ministry for the benefit of residents was started and most successfully carried on by Norma Dryer, wife of Chaplain Walt. She started a ministry for women from over twenty churches to supply such handcrafted items for residents as afghans, lap robes, lap quilts, booties, wheelchair pillows, shawls, therapy balls, and chair arm caddies. She wrote an instruction manual called <u>Caring and Sharing</u> for distribution among the churches. Norma wrote letters, read to patients, brought flowers, and was family to those who had none; her cheerful countenance brightened every room she entered. She suffered a fatal stroke in October 1984. The loss was great for all who knew her, and was devastating for Walt and his family, but he quietly pursued his work in the midst of his grief.

Other Chaplains added were:
Lloyde Lowe, to serve in Rhode Island, assisted by his wife, Millie.
Dale Malone, to serve in Maine with his wife, Judy.

At the close of 1984, CCS was servicing two homes in Maine, ten in Massachusetts, and one in Rhode Island, with a total of 1,151 residents.

As for the financial base, there were now 211 contributors, 70 of them having been added in 1984 alone, with a weekly income of $983 and an income for the year of $51,138.

From his 1984 Annual Report, Dave states, "In early 1984 I felt from my perspective that CCS was entering a period of development and progress...the ensuing months have proven this to be true...I conclude that CCS has turned the corner and is going on to greater things."

He then expressed his deep appreciation to the Board and to the entire staff for their hard work, for their harmonious support emotionally, spiritually, and financially, and for their prayers and encouragement. These efforts by his co-workers had been key elements in every sense in helping to turn the corner.

Chapter Thirteen

WALT

Again, at a strategic time in Dave's deputation he was to meet a man who had a heart for the elderly. Walt Dryer's experience follows in his own words.

"I heard of CCS through David's visit to my office in 1979. He came asking for a meeting.

"Nursing Home ministry was part of my pastoral work at Calvary Baptist in Claremont, New Hampshire. I had some of my members in the local county home, and visited them on Wednesday afternoons. On one occasion I was approached by the administrator and his wife, who asked if I would be interested in being the Protestant chaplain, the former chaplain having retired. At the time I could not even consider it because of the demands of a growing congregation. In addition to a full slate of services (both a morning and evening service, Sunday school, and prayer meeting, all of which needed weekly preparation), we had started a Christian school, with which I was deeply involved as administrator. I suggested to the administrator of the home that he might ask one of the twenty-three other Protestant pastors in town, many of whom had only the Sunday morning service. But he soon repeated his request, saying that they had contacted all the pastors and all were too busy. He did not hear protestations of being too busy myself, which I was. He cited the fact that I was the only pastor coming, and coming regularly.

"I promised that I would speak to my deacons about it, thinking that surely they would not want me to get involved further. But in the meeting, one deacon encouraged it as a testimony. If I would do it, they promised to help.

"As the chaplain, I started visitation each Wednesday on all Protestant residents. The following week, I started to hear residents who were not

Protestant calling to me from their rooms. After a couple of weeks I spoke of my frustration at this, at which the administrator said I could visit all residents if I wished. This formed in my mind the direction of the ministry that I was soon to follow with CCS.

"When David visited our church, my heart was moved. His simple showing of slides of nursing homes brought home to me the possibility of a full-time ministry there. Helping him pack up, I remarked that sometime, after I retire, I would be interested in a nursing home ministry full-time. David's simple remark was, 'Walt, we need you now!'

"Correspondence followed, as I planned to follow the call that I was sure the Lord had given. I applied to CCS. But there were obstacles. We were building a large addition to the church. Our school had blossomed, increasing my responsibilities. My youngest daughter was nearing high school graduation. In addition, we had no means of support, and I now found myself struggling with the idea, so often expressed, that *God's work done in God's way will not lack God's supply*.

"But then things started to come together. The school was running well, the building addition was completed, my daughter was graduated from our Christian school and had gone into a brief time of service with a Christian singing group, and the possibility of an interim pastoral position opened.

"I finally made my decision, probably the hardest of my life, to leave the pastorate I loved to step out on faith into a ministry where there were few guidelines. I had often reassured my young people that if the Lord called them to serve Him, they could trust Him to supply their needs. Now it was my turn to prove it, and I confess that I struggled.

"Our church, however, was a great help to us. That year we had voted that any missionary the church supported would receive at least 10 percent of their support from the church if they were members, and 5 percent if not members. There were seven young people moving out into Christian service that year, and we had expended our missions budget. We could expect nothing. But at their business meeting it was suggested that if the pastor could set out on faith, the church ought to be able to, also. They, on faith, picked up 10 percent of our support (and have never missed a payment).

"When we moved into the interim pastorate, and I started part-time in the nursing homes, I knew that the Lord had indeed directed, and that I was in the place of God's choosing. Through the thirteen years I have served the Lord with CCS this has been confirmed again and again. And, together with this confirmation, God's promise to supply our needs has been proven."

As with Chaplain Havumaki, God again did the choosing. Dave had gone to Walt hoping to set up a meeting at the church from which might come support for CCS. The leading was correct, but God had a greater purpose. Walt's ministry with CCS has been invaluable, both as a chaplain and as Executive Director upon Dave's retirement.

Chapter Fourteen
THE INHERITANCE

Dave had another special lady in his life besides me: his stepmother, Ida. Ida had come into our lives, and especially Dave's, in the late Fifties. We had known her for years before that time and could not have been more delighted at Dad K's choice of "the lady in his life," several years after Dave's mother had died. Dave would have been a terribly spoiled little boy had Ida been his mom! She delighted in championing him, and I loved them both enough not to mind. She was a devout believer, and a successful business woman; she had a lovely singing voice, and was pretty enough to steal the show from the bride at a wedding when she was in her late seventies.

Six years after we moved to 14 Greenbrier Drive, Ida was discharged from the Lahey Clinic with a diagnosis of inoperable cancer. We had the room to take her home and it was our privilege to have her with us and to care for her for her several remaining months, until the degree of care made it necessary for her to be moved to a twenty-four hour care facility.

One day at the nursing home I found her looking very distressed, and I said, "You're troubled."

She replied, "Yes, I am. I am worried about your mortgage. Tell David I want to talk to him." I did that, and he went to see her the following day. Ida, in her strong, take-charge voice said, "David, I want your mortgage paid, and I want you to call my attorney and have him make all the necessary arrangements to pay it." Her mind was made up, as only Ida's could be, so Dave did as she asked, and in a very brief time it was done.

We could hardly believe it was happening—after only six years our home was debt-free! What a wonderful Lady and substitute Mother, and what a wonderful event in our lives!

"Oh yes, Lord, now we do remember, back in Minnesota when we first read your instructions to Abraham, there was a promise to him that we missed at the time. It said, 'And Abraham obeyed...not knowing where he was going...*To a place he was to receive for an inheritance with his heirs.'* There it was, Lord, but we never saw it! You had it in mind all along!"

Indeed, what a good God!

Perhaps one reason God let us miss the promise at that time was that we might not have kept our priorities straight. We humans so easily get sidetracked, especially when tempted by things, and it might have been very easy to run ahead of Him. God truly had been the Architect and Builder of the entire venture which started in 1973 and brought us to this point in time, 1982.

Chapter Fifteen
DECADE TWO

The years from 1985 to 1994 brought several changes to CCS, plus many additions.

The first major change was the resignation of Dave Kimball as Executive Director, effective as of 1986. He no longer felt physically able to produce as he knew was necessary to see steady growth, and while he backed away reluctantly, his words to the Board reflected his optimism and confidence as he looked forward: "I am firmly and enthusiastically convinced that Walt Dryer was brought to us not only for his very fine chaplain ministry, but now to take up the leadership of the work and move it on to broader and improved effectiveness. I thank God for the day He led me to Claremont, New Hampshire, to be in touch with His man."

His man, Walt Dryer, took on the new challenge, to the complete satisfaction of the entire Board. His duties included, among others, overseeing the work of the various chaplains, raising funds and managing the office, traveling extensively to publicize the work of the chaplains, and preparing them for their assignments with brief training programs in understanding and assisting the elderly, particularly those dealing with problems and handling grief. Under his leadership the work went on to exciting new dimensions.

The next change came with Walter Peterson's resignation due to failing health. This very wise and dedicated man had been an inspiration to Dave since 1974; he had been the first Board member, and the first Chairman of the Board. His absence left a huge vacancy, both on the Board and for Dave personally.

The existing Board maintained an attitude of constant vigilance for individuals who could make valuable contribution to the policy-setting process.

New additions during this decade were:
   Rev. Don Hoaglund, Manchester, New Hampshire
   Mr. Robert Jackson, Plymouth, Massachusetts
   Rev. Harry Egner, Waterford, Connecticut
   Mr. Douglas Hale, Middleboro, Massachusetts

Mr. William Capezio, Barrington, Rhode Island
Mr. David Chamberlain, W. Bridgewater, Massachusetts
Mrs. Greer Lyon, Middletown, Rhode Island
Dr. Eric Sweitzer, Middleboro, Massachusetts
Mr. James Creamer, Norton, Massachusetts
Mr. Al Whitaker, Lakeville, Massachusetts

But the very newest addition to CCS was a new Mrs. Walt Dryer! Walt's semi-annual report in '86 says:

"My forthcoming marriage is something for which I am truly grateful. Living has not been easy for me, and I look forward to Shirley's help and companionship. She is well prepared for sharing my ministry, and will provide a well-ordered home, and love that I have greatly missed."

Shirley is a special lady; pretty, gracious, and energetic. She is a scrupulous homemaker and, with her gift of hospitality, she combines the two for the benefit of others, especially in her service to CCS. I remember Walt's calling one day after a trip to Connecticut and mentioning to me that he had met a lovely lady, he felt so comfortable with her, etc., etc., whereupon I said, like the true romantic that I am, "Aha!" (I felt also like a mother-confessor). July 26th was about the warmest day of summer for their friends to join them for their day and then send them on to Word of Life Chalet at Schroon Lake, New York, for their honeymoon. A 1995 update from Walt says that the above is an understatement, and that it gets better every day!

Things have a way of getting back to normal, however, and so the work resumed. Noteworthy items of interest include the following:

- **Annual Dinner instituted.**
- **Membership in "Evangelical Council for Financial Accountability" established.**
- **Permission granted by the major tract companies for their tracts to be enlarged on CCS copier.**
- **"Associate chaplain" category (chaplains otherwise employed but working part-time with CCS) added.**
- **Large print "Our Daily Bread" supplied at no cost for all chaplains by Radio Bible Class (regarded as the best piece of literature for evangelism, comfort, and Christian nurture).**
- **Computer, software, copier, plus money for training and maintenance donated by Digital Corp.**
- **Various music groups performing as guests at several homes.**
- **Annual Fall seminars scheduled, starting in 1990.**
- **The Sonshine Society's provision of free large print Scripture portions.**

- **Annual income exceeded $100,000 for the first time, 1989.**
- **Donation of WordPerfect 6.0 software for the computer.**
- **Chaplains added during the decade were:**
  Rev. William Paige, Concord, New Hampshire
  Mrs. Kay Fries, Lititz, Pennsylvania (ret. '89)
  Rev. David Schaffer, Fairhaven, Massachusetts and his wife, Ruth.
  Rev. Mel Hatcher, St. Petersburg, Florida
  Rev. Cliff Olson, Jay, Maine, and his wife, Wilma
  Rev. W. Lee Hause, Lancaster, Pennsylvania and his wife, Arlene.
  Rev. Ivan Crossman, Sherburne Falls, Massachusetts
- **Associate Chaplains added were:**
  Mrs. Elsie Cordis, Suffield, Connecticut
  Mr. Ted Durgin and wife June, Newport, Rhode Island
  Miss Helen Berry, St. Petersburg, Florida
  Mr. Darwin Ransom, Barre, Vermont and his wife, Joan.
  Mr. Bob Collins, Honey Brook, Pennsylvania
  Mr. Brain Arold, Owasco, New York
  Mr. Thomas Ryder, Chadds Ford, Pennsylvania
  Mr. Lynwood Comstock, Westport, Massachusetts
  Mrs. Chris Ferguson, No. Dartmouth, Massachusetts
  Mr. Bill Cain, W. Bridgewater, Massachusetts.
  Mr. Steve Woodward, Southbury, Connecticut
  Mr. Harvey Pierce, Rochester, Massachusetts and his wife, Lorraine.
  Mrs. Adele Offringa, Wareham, Massachusetts
  Mrs. June Durgin, Carver, Massachusetts who replaced her husband, Ted, who went Home to be with the Lord.

At the close of 1994 progress is evidenced by the following facts:

The annual income reached $176,595; over thirty chaplains now serve in the six New England States, New York, New Jersey, Pennsylvania, Georgia, Florida, and five in New Brunswick, Canada; these chaplains in 1994, made 74,000 personal visits, held 330 services, and registered 130 decisions for faith in our Savior.

In his annual report Walt states:

"Nineteen ninety-four was a momentous year for CCS—our chaplain staff growing by 50 percent to 30+; a successful transfer to in-house accounting; two successful banquets; two opportunities with national exposure; our Canada affiliate moving forward in a significant way; and finally, a skilled part-time secretary in the office, Mrs. Evelyn Staples, with expertise in computers, to augment the faithful labors of Mrs. Ethel Sturgis, who has worked gratis for these many years.

The unsolicited publicity at the Conservative Baptist Annual Meeting in Minneapolis in June, involving Walt's invitation to address the 700 National Delegates concerning nursing home chaplains, and the front page spread on the chaplain publication, <u>Front Line</u>, gave much needed exposure for the chaplain ministry among conservative Baptists. The status of nursing home chaplains was advanced to the level of military chaplains, in the sense that all are included under the umbrella of chaplain ministries of the Conservative Baptists. Those meetings, plus the Sonshine Society rally in Cleveland in September 1994 where Walt gave a seminar on "The Place of the Professional Chaplaincy in Nursing Homes," have brought many inquiries, and have created fresh interest in CCS.

Along with his full year at the office, Walt made several extended deputation trips, as well as one each to New Jersey, New Hampshire, Vermont, and to New Brunswick, Canada. The chaplains' in-service seminar, designed to inform the chaplains regarding their ministry needs, has been extended to three days. Subjects covered over the past six years include:

1989 Accountability and Faithfulness
1990 Death and Dying
1991 Alzheimer's Disease
1992 Right-to-Die Issues
1993 The Art of Listening
1994 Sharpening Witnessing Skills

A vision for the future includes a permanent home for CCS, suitable not only for office space but having accommodations for visiting chaplains during training and seminars. There is also the need for the continuous upgrading of the entire computer system along with adequate staff.

There is the need for wisdom in securing the Director of God's choice to replace Walt upon his retirement in 1996.

And, finally, there is a need to catch the attention of upcoming generations and to challenge them regarding their possible role in *grandparent awareness* in our fractured society. The same challenge should extend to the ever-increasing field for Christian vocations in nursing homes in the areas of administrators, social workers, chaplains, nurses and other caregiving professions.

"How, Lord, do we implement all of this? Give special direction, please, as you have consistently done since the beginning of this CCS venture, and place your Hand upon the *whomevers* out there, who can give of themselves that others may be receptive to your Gospel."

Chapter Sixteen
CARING AND SHARING

April of 1988 saw the continuation of the ministry that had been dormant since the homegoing of Norma Dryer, that of handmade articles for the residents of nursing homes. Ruth Schaffer, wife of Chaplain David, was asked by Walt to assume the responsibility and Ruth picks up the story in her own words:

"By the time I took over this project, we really did have a closetful of items to give to our residents.

"How did we acquire all these things? Whenever Walt or David presented the work at various churches, we would have a display: tracts, handmade articles, and the pattern booklets <u>Caring and Sharing</u> which I have edited and are now in their fourth printing. Many women would be attracted to the handmade articles and feel that was something they could do to help the ministry. So from churches all around New England and occasionally from other states, packages arrived or were picked up when we were in the area.

"How do I go about distributing these gifts? I give an itemized list to the activities director and she puts in a request for the number of each item that she thinks would be desired in that home. I check my supplies, prepare the order, and call her to set up a delivery time. On the day of delivery, one of the workers goes with me through the corridors with a rolling cart stacked as high as possible, and we meet each resident to determine what he/she would like. This allows the resident to pick out a particular color or style, which makes it very personal, and I mark the name on the item whenever possible.

"Some residents say that this is better than Christmas because the items are very useful in their daily living. I am also given other small items such as crocheted crosses, pen holders, tissue holders and toilet articles that I can give to those who have no need for any of the other items. We want everyone to feel happy and for no one to feel left out.

"What are some of the reactions of the residents? Many cannot believe that it is *free*. They say, 'Nothing is free anymore!' Then they find it hard to believe that someone who doesn't even know them has taken the time to make such a beautiful lap quilt or whatever it may be. I do give them a small gift card that says it is from Community Chaplain Service and made by a Christian friend in the name of our Lord Jesus Christ. Since some residents cannot remember or respond, the cards are also helpful in letting the family know from whom the gifts came.

"A lady may have a towel around her shoulders and when given a lovely shawl she is full of thanks—sometimes tears. Recently I had a gentleman burst into tears when given a lap quilt: he had been sitting in a chair with a sheet over his knees.

"Occasionally the resident or the family member of a resident will take the time to send a lovely thank-you note. This week I received one from a 90-year-old lady who was thanking me for her walker bag and then she included thanks for the items that her friends had gotten! The handwriting was shaky, so I knew that it took a lot of effort and love to send that note.

"Some find it so hard to make up their minds, but we try to be very patient and help them make a decision. Not all are old. Recently a mother was so grateful for a lap quilt for her son who is confined to a wheelchair. It provided extra warmth when she took him outside for a breath of fresh air.

"Many of the nurses appreciate the gifts. When the residents are in the hallways or a dayroom and they are covered with the brightly colored lap robes, it is not only cheery to see them, but they look nicely covered, as well.

"There are other items that we distribute in the homes. Tray favors for any and all holidays are made by older ladies in mission circles and by children in Sunday school or vacation Bible school. Some make greetings cards. How they love to get Valentines made by children!

"A lady in her nineties makes scrapbooks from old magazines. She could knit or crochet in years past, but then felt there was nothing more she could do. Someone gave her the idea of making the scrapbooks. Now she is continuing to serve the Lord and she is happy. The homes appreciate the books. The pictures help the residents remember everyday occurrences or help them to recall stories about their past. The picture of a doll may bring back memories of a doll she once had—perhaps the *only* doll she ever had and at great sacrifice to her parents because those were Depression days.

"Another woman is very much involved in crocheting. She found out about our work through a friend of a friend. Her husband was shut in, then her son was with her, and required care. Through it all, she said it was wonderful therapy for her, and was even better because she knew it was helping somebody else. What a blessing to see how the Lord fits all the pieces together.

"How does this relate to my husband's ministry? It is amazing how receiving a gift will change the attitude of a resident. One who did not care to talk with him now is interested in his message. God uses these gifts to open doors and hearts. How wonderful!

"The ministry has grown. During the course of a year I give away hundreds of handmade items and a thousand and more small items like the tray favors, lapel pins, cards, etc. Now when the other chaplains come for the annual seminar in the fall I urge them to go to the closet and take as much as they desire. We know that this is spreading the ministry—even to Canada. We are grateful that God can use the smallest gift to bring glory to Himself."

Chapter Seventeen
EARL

From high up under the rafters of Boston Garden came another of those typical outbursts from that same fan, the sort of outburst that caused ladies and even mildly sensitive men to blush. The perpetrator was one Earl Hodgkins, man without God, mixologist (bartender), night-club combo drummer, hockey fanatic. Listen as Earl tells his own story:

"My life certainly was not shaped by the few times I attended Sunday School, and because I went by myself my parents never knew that I further abbreviated my time spent in religious training so as to leave my collection money intact for ice cream on the way home. I was never taken to church. Upon graduation from high school in 1943 I entered the U.S. Navy and served as a medical corpsman for three years in a variety of overseas locations, and after receiving my discharge I was employed for five years as a salesclerk, followed by fifteen years with the American District Telegraph Company until my Christian training.

"In 1952 I married my wife, Joan, and continued my practice of annually acquiring my season ticket for the Boston Bruins. Boston Garden became by church, and I was there every time the doors were open for a hockey game along with my fellow worshippers, contributing to the atmosphere from my considerable vocabulary and enjoying the reactions I observed around me in response to my verbal improprieties. At one Christmas season game, four young ladies who sat in front of us at the games presented me with a gift, allegedly from Milt Schmidt, but it was really from the girls. The gift was a very large dog muzzle, a strong hint to me to clean up my act! My wife had already stopped attending with me for obvious reasons, after administering many strong jabs to my ribs to no avail.

"During those years our daughter, Elaine, was born, and due to her fierce loyalty to her daddy who did not like church, she decided she did not like church either and conveniently became ill just in time to stay home, with an immediate improvement in her health as soon as her mother left by herself.

"My musical trio played for just about any kind of celebration. I was usually the master of ceremonies and our group could easily have been called the 'any-excuse-to-have-a-party' group. Joan no longer went with me and I was finding many temptations which had never been a problem before. After nine years of being together, we began experiencing serious marital difficulties. Her renewed fellowship with the Lord and her church had given me another cause to display my vocabulary, and the widening rift between us led to our seeking counseling through a community family service.

"I was advised by the marriage counselor to try attending church with my wife in an attempt for us to seek some sort of goals going in the same direction. I agreed to go, and I heard the Gospel, along with the testimonies of those whose lives had been changed by salvation through the blood of Jesus Christ. Joan asked for prayer for me, and her pastor, Gordon J. Kirk, and two other local pastors met regularly to pray for my salvation. I firmly believe that at the time Joan asked prayer for me and showed in her life a real concern for our marriage, God began working on me, and it was those prayers, and the concern for this sinner, which paved the way for my conversion.

"One of those pastors invited me to a Christian Business Men's supper in Brockton, Massachusetts, on January 22, 1962. Chuck Harwood of the Heinz Company of New England gave his testimony that evening, and I was deeply convinced of my sin and my need for salvation. At the invitation to receive Christ, I quietly did just that, and, at that moment, my B.C. (before Christ) days were over!

"The transition period from the old to the new was quick and powerful. The night of my conversion as I sat at home in the quiet of the living room I picked up the hymnal from the piano and God led my fingers to the back where the Responsive Readings were. I had no idea what they were, but the pages stopped at a reading entitled *Strong Drink*. I read it through, found out from Joan that it was in the Bible, and the Lord made it clear immediately that I must end my bartending! The following day I visited both establishments where I had served liquor and resigned my position, first explaining to the owners what the Lord's saving grace had done for me the night before, and inviting them both, as best as I knew how, to get saved also. They declined, but I know that I have the respect of one of them to this day. Along with all this my drum-playing also became a thing of the past.

"To further augment my earnings after giving up my extra jobs, I went into a partnership with a new Christian friend. We tithed the business faithfully, the Lord blessed it, and consequently some time later, when the need arose for extra funds for college, my partner bought me out. That money helped immensely with my tuition until the end of my college days. His widow faithfully sends us a widow's mite to support our work to this day!

"Through the faithful discipling of Pastor Kirk, I grew steadily in my love for the Lord and in the knowledge of His Word, and experienced the restoration of joy in my marriage. Following Baptism and church membership, I became involved with ministries within the church and with the Christian Businessmen's Committee, and acquired a growing desire to be a good witness for the Lord. At a Christmas Eve service in the church, the Lord spoke to both of us about full-time service in the pastorate. While we made preparations and sought His will as to schooling, we gained more experience by serving in local nursing homes and senior citizens' ministries.

"In September 1964, at the age of thirty-nine, I began my studies at the Philadelphia College of the Bible. I can imagine that at least forty of my former drinking buddies fell off their bar stools when they heard that one! During that time I served as youth director in the Southwest Presbyterian Church in Philadelphia, for a period of three and a half years. In the spring of 1968, I graduated with a bachelor of science degree in Bible and began my ministry as pastor of the Calvary Baptist Church in Westfield, Maine. It was my practice there as well as in two subsequent pastorates to lead our members into regular nursing home and rest home ministries. Most of these are ongoing to this day. My final ministry was at Peoples' Church, Truro, Nova Scotia, Canada, where one of the deacons heads and establishes works on a regular basis in local nursing homes, involving many members and Bible school students.

"Although I resigned that pastorate in September 1990 (having reached that turning point age of sixty-five), the word retirement had no place in my vocabulary in spite of a leg problem. I felt deeply that the God who had called me to pastor twenty-six years earlier would have to show me very definitely if I was to discontinue that calling. In the months that followed I awaited His leading *somewhere*, but although many key people knew of my situation, I did not hear from one church, not even to be an interim or a pulpit supplier. To be very honest, that does not enlarge a man's ego, but I definitely got the message!

"About that time my wife had taken a trip to visit family in Massachusetts, and it was her usual habit to attend the West Bridgewater

Baptist Church with her sisters. While there she had become acquainted with David Chamberlain, who was a member of the Board of Directors of the Community Chaplain Service located in New Bedford. David knew that my heart had always leaned strongly towards nursing homes, and that all my pastorates had included a ministry in that area. It was David who gave my wife some information about CCS, and some literature to take home for me to peruse. After reading it, I decided to write for more in-depth information, which led me to arrange an interview for my wife and me with Walter Dryer during our Christmas visit to the States.

"When the Lord is in a thing He makes it happen! We did not have to hurry back to Truro as my resignation was in effect, so early in January, Joan and I went to New Bedford to meet Walter, who carefully explained in detail CCS's position and performance. I visited a home with Chaplain David Schaffer, and by the end of our visit, and with much prayer, we knew the door was open for us to become a part of CCS.

"Things happened quickly! We felt no leading to return to the States to live, and CCS was most gracious in suggesting that we begin our chaplaincy in Canada. During those days in the States our home in Truro sold. And the Lord even takes care of our ego for upon our return to Truro to prepare to move we heard from four churches that were looking for a pastor. But we were already signed in with CCS. God's timing is never wrong!

"Thus began the great challenge of planting (I like the word 'pioneering') another chapter of CCS, this time in the Maritime Provinces of Canada, and here I was, at retirement age, with the responsibility of introducing a new and relatively unknown ministry to my part of the world!"

Chapter Eighteen
CCS CANADA

Entering the third decade brings CCS into new and exciting times and to a repeat of the same theme: that of God having in place the person He desires to use to further what He has begun, when He is ready to do so.

Earl Hodgkins was to be the person, the starting place would be the Rothesay Baptist Church in New Brunswick, Canada. When Earl made his first contact with pastor John Boyd, the immediate response was, "What can we do to help you?" He was as good as his word. After a meeting between John, Walt Dryer, the church board, and Earl, it was decided that the mission would come under the *umbrella* of the Rothesay church, which offered office space, the means to receive funds from supporting churches and individuals, and much encouragement!

Earl states: "We cannot begin to recount the number of individuals who helped the new chapter to make inroads into Canada. On our very first visit to a tiny little church in Upper Hampstead, New Brunswick, the pastor's wife, Jean Nickerson, introduced us to Robert Corbett, acting administrator, and his wife, Laverne, the director of nursing, of the Woolastook Nursing Home in the town of Gagetown, New Brunswick, who have been most gracious and helpful. Our ministry in that home began that very first week! Pastor Gerry Nickerson and his wife wonderfully aided us in keeping the work going, spending many hours making copies of tracts, forms, reports, and other vital papers for us, for we didn't even own a typewriter for the mission yet!

"Deputation is an interesting word, and is a familiar one to pastors, because many prospective missionaries in seeking to raise support to speed them to their fields of service send numerous letters and make many telephone calls to churches, asking for the opportunity to present their call, their mission, and their needs. Deputation now became a password! From the role of pastor, I now became one of those eager missionaries, the main difference being a wide age gap! Most missionaries start their careers much earlier in life, many as graduates fresh from a Bible school. Seeking to raise adequate financial support and to line up meetings to present the work became a very exciting and very interesting learning experience for this 65-year-old recruit!

"As Walter would say, I was quite aggressive, and went to work quickly, contacting churches all over the Maritimes and in the eastern regions of the States. Our approach was to come and preach the Word, and present the work, and the Lord graciously provided a very high percentage of responses to our inquiries. Having been a pastor was in my favor, and as we successfully set up a full calendar of dates, we adapted ourselves to lugging suitcases and equipment to far-off places, acquainting ourselves with new congregations and renewing fellowship with former ones, sleeping in all types of beds and situations, and learning to eat things we did not normally eat. This deputation-thing became an experience we will never regret, and God was so good to us!

"Learning how to interest people in a nursing home ministry is not easy, and it is certainly not the most exciting form of missions, but the Lord provided us with some helpful tools. We had a real burden to produce a slide presentation that would honor the Lord, capture the hearts of people, and present the elderly in their need, *with dignity*. Many miles were traveled, and it was on one such trip while listening to tapes that we found just the right song to use as background music. We secured permission to use it, then barnstormed with photographers Ron and Susan Richard of Truro, and Pastor Nickerson, and put together a presentation which was written and narrated by Joan.

"A member of a church in one of the northernmost towns of Maine learned of my need of a slide projector and presented us with a brand-new one still in the original box! From two individuals in two different states came two separate checks marked *For the typewriter*, and they exactly covered the purchase price. God works in wondrous ways!

"During our travels over the roads for four years in deputation God gave us experiences too numerous to mention here. Prayer partners ranged from the wee to the elderly, financial supporters gave from the widow's mite upwards to larger gifts, and children gave us their own personal stuffed animals or dolls for someone in a home to love. Over one hundred signed up to pray for a specific home resident upon receiving a small profile of the need. We spent many hours in correspondence keeping prayer partners updated, and thanking them for their concerns.

"While we carried on that part of our mission, Walt Dryer made several trips to St. John, where he made contact with the Rothesay Baptist pastor and other individuals about prospective Board members. Much prayer was offered to God for direction, and for the establishing of CCS as a fully accredited, wholly Canadian Mission. Mr. Dexter Stultz, business administrator of Rothesay Baptist Church, helped greatly with his organizational skills. In His time the Lord knit together a committed group of men and women to serve as members of the Board. We were fully established as a non-profit organization in '93. Mr. Ken Anthony became our Board Chairman and, under his earnest efforts and with cooperation from the Board, Community Chaplain Service gained recognition among the churches and nursing homes. Opportunities to serve opened everywhere, and my burden leaned heavily toward recruiting more chaplains.

"There was also a new awareness in congregations: a young couple began bringing their musical instruments to a home for weekly one-on-one visits; a burdened pastor challenged his people, which resulted in over twenty-five members inviting us to present a two-hour seminar on how to visit, then breaking up into groups and visiting five or six different homes; some pastors admitted finding this a difficult part of their ministry and asked for help. These were all sweet added blessings!

"During the early part of 1994, the Lord suggested to us that we needed to slow down and leave the road work to younger, more physically able men and women. Our decision to become part-time chaplains appears to have opened the door to would-be chaplains, because we soon added five more, namely:

Terry Johnston, Rothesay, New Brunswick
Stewart Moen, Halifax, Nova Scotia
Gayle Dow, St. John, New Brunswick
Charles Bramble, Gagetown, New Brunswick
Michelle Barker, Student Chaplain, St. John, New Brunswick

"Thus we left our deputation years and moved to White Head Island, off the east coast of Grand Manan, where the Lord had prepared a loving church to receive us, help us build a home, and minister to us. We settled into weekly visits in the Grand Manan Nursing Home where, as June says, the lounge full of residents crowned with white heads of hair truly indicate that the field really is white unto harvest!

"Back on White Head there are also many senior citizens, younger couples, and even teens who feel they can come and share with us, seek our counsel, and just ask for our prayers. I have a new name for myself: *minister-at-large!*"

CCS Canada has now appointed Chaplain Terry Johnston as assistant director temporarily for 1995. Besides his weekly visits in three homes, he will be going on the road to promote the work wherever the Lord opens the door, and will seek other men and/or women to accept the challenge to be chaplains.

> ∾ **Along with Mr. Ken Anthony, Chairman, other board members are:**
> Mr. David Wade, Vice-chairman, Hampton, New Brunswick
> Mr. Alan Atherton, Treasurer, Hatfield Point, New Brunswick
> Mrs. Diana Wade, Secretary, Hampton, New Brunswick
> Rev. E. Lloyd Lake, St. John, New Brunswick
> Ms. Kate Coffman, St. John, New Brunswick
> Rev. John Boyd, Rothesay, New Brunswick
> Rev. John Fancy, Rothesay, New Brunswick
>   (U.S. Director and Board chairman, ex-officio).

Aggressive promotion on TV, seminars, and speaking engagements have all been utilized to better acquaint the Maritime area with the CCS ministry. The obvious leading of God, the hundreds who faithfully prayed, the energetic and capable leadership of Board chairman Ken Anthony, Walt, the Boards, and the chaplains in the States are all key ingredients in the success of this venture.

On June third, 1995, CCS-Canada had their very own first annual banquet! It was a wonderful evening of celebration in honor of Earl and Joan Hodgkins with 120 enthusiastic supporters of the entire CCS ministry in attendance. Considering the positive outlook exhibited there we conclude that CCS-Canada is indeed alive and well!

Through the fellowship of the annual seminars and banquets the chaplains experience a sense of belonging to a family, though they are separated by the many miles which lie between Florida and New Brunswick. The cohesiveness of the group is heart-warming and their zest is contagious. There is an excitement among the chaplains that emanates not only from an ever-increasing knowledge of the God who is, and what He has done for mankind, but also from a value system that has become more finely tuned over the years. Solid things have been sorted out from among the mundane and trivial. Eternity has become the joyous and anticipated goal at the end of the journey. Love is for sharing. These truths they know for sure and when it comes to sharing them, these chaplains shine!

Chapter Nineteen
CHAPLAINS

And while we are on the subject, what are the requirements for being a good chaplain? Much has been learned over the past two decades and Executive Director Walt Dryer has this to say: "In the few years that I have been working with a special group of committed Christians who are nursing home chaplains, I have come to the conclusion that there are several qualities that they possess that I think must be present in a good chaplain."

Obviously, gender is not a factor. Each is valued for his or her distinctive gifts and skills.

We shall begin by answering a question with another question, that being, "What's in your heart?"

First and foremost, Jesus must be in a chaplain's heart through a personal experience of salvation, accompanied by the love of God which can only be given through the Holy Spirit (Romans 5:5). The heart must also have in residence a personal warmth and caring for others, accompanied by a sense of urgency that others know Him, too. One might assume that a degree in theology is a necessary prerequisite. Not so. A degree from a most prestigious school would be of little use if one's heart is cool toward elements of human need.

Conversely, a caring and all-embracing spirit is inadequate if there are insufficient skills in imparting God's answers to questions relating to His love, and to His provisions for eternity. So there is the need for competency in the use of relevant Scriptures for dealing adequately with those who are to be helped to know Him, or who need His assurance, His encouragement or His comfort.

Innate sensitivity and understanding for the sick and elderly are valuable factors. Patience, a natural trait for some people and for others an acquired virtue, is a must in dealing with all sorts of situations common to infirmities and advanced years. All of these capabilities can be enhanced by the use of training seminars and reading materials.

A sense of humor is paramount, both for the benefit of the residents, and for the chaplain. Many residents probably have scant cause to laugh; one chaplain finds simple jokes to be effective tools when used sensitively. But after hours of visiting, the chaplain may handle the events of the day in a healthier fashion if his or her own sense of humor is intact and functioning well!

A cheerful heart, yet one that does not seem to make light of the residents' plight, can sometimes turn them to more positive attitudes. And don't forget the warmth and caring that can be expressed by touching; when did they last feel a hug? Authorities say everyone should have at least ten hugs a day!

Seemingly small segments of time, perhaps sacrificially given, can bring great comfort into these lives, and the skills of a concert pianist or an operatic soprano are not necessary in order to touch their hearts. Nursing home residents are, for the most part, appreciative and undemanding, and their expectations are simple. A few moments spent playing and singing some of the old hymns, for instance, might encourage a smile and even an attempt to sing, and no one would mind at all if the voices quavered and cracked! Picture one little lady in a home who sang one song, all day long, in the same little birdlike voice: "Take Me Out to the Ballgame." She was absolutely delighted if someone came in and sang a verse with her; her eyes did not open, but she knew someone was there; you could tell by the expression on her face!

Reading is a simple yet valuable ministry. Many residents have suffered strokes and have lost all ability with words, except to listen. Short stories, letters, books, and hometown newspaper articles of special interest all contribute enormously to their lives. Reading their cards to them is special; many times the staff just does not have the time to follow through with this extra task.

Writing letters, notes, and thank-you cards for a gift received can be a service much appreciated by the resident and often by the family as well. Sometimes these chores can be tedious, but they come under the heading of "sacrifice for His sake."

Treats are a big item! One dear lady asked, almost before her visitor could sit down by her, "Did you bring something?" Her favorite wish was for ice cream, and it made her day. For those subjected to dietary restrictions, small gift items can tell them that they are special and are not alone.

Many times the greatest service is just to be a good listener (and there are not many of them around: try finding one for yourself); let residents find relief and release from tensions by telling you all the things they have on their minds, when no one else seems to have time to listen.

One of the most excited CCS chaplains lives her whole life and carries out her ministry from a wheelchair. She is received by the nursing home staff with open arms, and as she visits with patients, her chair becomes an instant equalizer: it signifies that she, too, is dealing with something she would not choose to have in her life, and that just perhaps she might understand "some of my feelings." It is also a valuable asset because it automatically provides eye-level contact, and, of course, she never has to go looking for a chair, which is often a scarce commodity in a nursing home!

CCS chaplains are trained before their commissioning. They are not expected to step out on their own and attempt to minister without being given the tools to aid them in doing their job. One-on-one instruction with the director, plus on-the-job time with a seasoned chaplain help prepare the candidate for entering what may be a totally new field of endeavor.

Because the financial base requires that the chaplain underwrite his ministry by deputizing his own funds, there should be in place those contacts with individuals, churches, or pastors which will assure that the necessary funding can be supplied. Practical suggestions for implementing this venture which would be new to most applicants can be supplied by headquarters.

Following is an easy reference list of these qualifications as stated by Director Walt:

1. *A personal experience of salvation through Christ.*
2. *The love of Christ in the heart (Romans 5:5).*
3. *A genuine love for the elderly, including the sick.*
4. *A good knowledge of elderly ways and needs.*
5. *A commitment to the work of ministry and raising support.*
6. *A willingness to sacrifice for Christ's sake.*
7. *A warm friendliness and generous spirit.*
8. *Ability to adapt and change.*
9. *Plenty of patience.*
10. *A sense of humor.*

And of course, it goes without saying, but I will say it anyway: the bottom line is, the chaplains are the keys to the success of the entire CCS ministry!

Chapter Twenty
NANA AND GRAMPA

As to my own regard for the elderly and their spiritual needs, I must refer back to my conversion and its impact on my family, especially my wonderful grandparents.

My big brother, Harry (known always as "Bud"), and I had been raised in part by Nana and Grampa after the divorce of our parents when we were very small. We lived with them in their cottage at the Lake for five years until the need for schooling made it necessary for us to move.

Our grandparents were very upright, God-fearing people who infused into our lives moral and ethical principles which have never left us. But I don't remember that I ever once heard the name of Jesus: profanity was not a part of our home, we had few opportunities to be with other folk, and the adults in our lives simply did not know who He was.

We had a unique life there: we learned to swim when very small; we roamed the wooded hillside known as Mt. Tom; we picked all kinds of berries; we fished (Bud was successful, I was not!); we sailed our little play boats on Pennamaquan Lake; we slid on our Flexible Flyer in winter; and we learned to love the call of the loons and the rain on the roof. We had a marvelous childhood, but such things do not last forever, and we did have to attend school, so when Bud was six and I was five we moved to the nearest town, West Pembroke. However, for most of our lives, every day that we could possibly manage it, we headed back to *Camp,* our name for the cottage to this day, to enjoy on an adult level the place of our roots.

West Pembroke was a charming little town nestled at the end of a tidal river extending in from Cobscook Bay. Its population at that time was about two hundred seventy-five, which included several famous sons. Among those were the Honorable Chief Justice William Pattengall of Maine's Supreme Court; former New Hampshire Governor and the United States Senator H. Styles Bridges, whose mother was to become our teacher;

and the local physician, Dr. Herbert Best, whose son, Charles, was to gain fame and recognition as a co-discoverer of insulin.

Dr. Best made his house calls in summer with one of three beautiful race horses hitched to a carriage. In winter the carriage was replaced by a pung, and memories of Dr. Best braving the frigid temperatures in a black bearskin coat, fur hat, and gloves, with snow flying from the horses' hooves as he hurried down the long country roads, can only be duplicated today on picture post cards. His remuneration often was a bushel of apples or potatoes, or a chicken or two.

His wife (known fondly as Lulu to adults in town—Mrs. Best to us children) one year made every child in town a round loaf of fruit-filled yeast bread, an English Christmas delicacy. Dr. Best taught us the names of Santa's reindeer, which I have never forgotten, and my brother remembers the day that Dr. Best gently reminded him that gentlemen take their hats off in the house!

It was a hard-working, industrious town with good solid citizens around us to set examples. There were numerous playmates in contrast to our isolation at Camp, and that tidal river ran directly behind our home for swimming if one was brave enough to challenge the water temperature. There were good books to borrow from neighbors, three at a time from Dr. Best who still had son Charlie's books in his office.

All in all, it was an especially nice place to grow up!

Our extraordinary teacher when we entered school was Mrs. Alina Bridges. Much could be said about this lady who had raised three very capable children—part of the time single-handedly—along with her teaching, but I will of necessity abbreviate.

We were expected to be obedient and respectful at school. For most of us, those requirements were merely a continuation of what was expected of us at home.

We marched proudly with our flag and "Head of Tide School" banner to Mrs. Bridges' direction as she beat out Left-right-Left-right on an empty chalk box with a rung of a defunct chair. Sometimes she used a hand-held school bell and beat time with the clapper, and on rainy days we marched up and down the aisles to "King Cotton," played on the phonograph which had to be wound up by a crank. Electric ones had not even been imagined yet! Little can be said for the stereophonics!

We learned our "tables" by rote (and it worked) and labored over Palmer Method Penmanship—"round and round, counter-clockwise, slip-slide, slip-slide."

Lights burned late. No one was considered ready for tomorrow's work until today's was understood and completed.

I remember going to the post office often for my mother just before five o'clock and seeing the lights still on in school, Mrs. Bridges bending over one of her 'scholars.'

In winter there were days when we sat in our boots and coats, and were sent up back to the big stove to get warm, row by row. However, our young janitor-helper's capabilities in the area of fire building left much to be desired so unless Mrs. Bridges was the fireman, the amount of heat emanating from said stove was minimal until mid-morning.

In spring we each tried to be the first to bring in lady's-slippers, mayflowers, and trilliums from the woods. And I can still recapture the joy of daydreaming as I gazed out the windows and watched the out-of-doors awaken as the snow and cold gave up their battle to dominate our lives.

Mrs. Bridges handled forty or so scholars in six grades in a one-room schoolhouse, built most of her own fires, did her own janitor work, and much more. With all of that, suffice it to say, we received more than a quality education!

One of the first things I learned was a dating system which separated events in history: B.C., before Christ, and A.D., in the year of our Lord. So my first awareness of this person, Christ, came at that time.

We started Sunday School and church attendance and of course the same name came into my life again. I developed a curiosity, childlike though it was, about who He was—this Jesus who died on a Cross, who was He, really? The answer to my question was always the same: a good man, a great teacher.

The mystery continued.

"But why did they kill Him?

I must not have asked someone who knew—many people don't—so the fact that He was God and that He gave Himself as my Atonement was to remain a mystery for the next several years.

I went on as a happy, active child not giving special attention to things spiritual, but always resting in the back of my mind was the suspicion that there was something about this mysterious Jesus that I did not know.

When teen years approached, my family moved again (Mother was remarried to a fine man), this time back to Eastport, the place of our birth. There I made new friends and among them were some who were special. They were normal, fun kids, active in school sports and church, and they even went to Prayer Meeting! I was impressed! After months of coaxing, I was finally given permission to attend the church where they attended, and there I learned the answer to my question, "Who is Jesus?" Jesus was God! And He died in my place for my sins! My immediate response was, "Why, of course!" Now it all made sense and in my heart I knew.

I rushed home to inform my family of this wonderful discovery of mine, but they were not in the least impressed. My mother's reply was, and I quote, "Young lady, there hasn't been a religious fanatic in this family for three generations that I know of and you aren't going to be the first. You forget this nonsense!"

I responded that I had finally found out who Jesus was and I could never forget Him. Thus, the predictable "era of conflict" settled into our lives that lasted for months, because I thought they would all finally come to believe because of my "much speaking."

God got me right out of the way by seeing to it that I went off to Providence Bible Institute, 500 miles away, and it came as a huge surprise to me to learn that He had not needed me at home at all, doing it all the wrong way. In fact, I learned that it was not even my responsibility to convince them. That was His responsibility. So I claimed the promise of Acts 16:31, "Believe on the Lord Jesus Christ and thou shalt be saved and thy house," and left them all there. Without me, mother, father, and brother all came to know Him.

After my first year at PBI, my eighty-year-old grampa told me that he did not understand this new faith of mine and he asked me to tell him what it was all about. I showed him a scripture verse about Salvation, probably John 3:16, though I do not remember precisely, and his response was, "How could Grampa have gone to church all his life and never heard this?" I had no answer other than my own experience but I asked him if he believed what he had read and he replied, "Of course I believe it, it's God's Word, but how did Grampa never see it before!" His heart was obviously so prepared and ready that he believed immediately.

Nana's first comment when Grampa told her about his discovery was, "Oh, Daddy, you're such a good man. How could God send you anywhere but to Heaven!" She resolutely disclaimed her need for a Saviour, and the following year she watched Grampa raise his arms toward Heaven and say, "Now, Lord Jesus, I'm all ready, come and get me." And his Lord came within the hour. When reminded of her spiritual need she would rock vigorously in her chair with lips pressed together and appear to shut us out. But little by little she began to speak very gently of "her Saviour" and of being in Heaven with Daddy and her little six-year-old son. She had finally accepted a substitute whose name was Jesus. She was eighty-eight when her new Saviour took her Home. Their graves in Hillside Cemetery in Eastport are marked simply "TIL HE COMES."

My memories of them are automatically linked to the many thousands out there who need a one-on-one chance to hear. Until now, a mere 1 percent of those over sixty-five have come to faith in Christ.

Chapter Twenty-one
OVERVIEW

The Community Chaplain Service ministry to the elderly is now on record, an ongoing established effort which is significantly appropriate for our day. Its vigor stands in sharp contrast to its somewhat moderate beginnings, and we stand reminded that God works not according to our recommendations and desires, but according to His sovereign timetable.

Growth in this decade includes the appointment of three new Board members, bringing the total to nine:

Rev. Stuart taylor, Middleboro, Massachusetts
Mr. John Baillie, Stoughton, Massachusetts
Mr. Ray Gramlich, New Bedford, Massachusetts

The staff stands at twenty-six in the United States and seven in Canada, figures which reflect retirements and those who for some reason found it necessary to become inactive, plus the following who have been recently appointed in the United States:

Rev. Alan Sutton, chaplain, Barrington, Rhode Island
Associate chaplains:
Dorothy Chase, North Dighton, Massachusetts
William Kelley, Tabernacle, New Jersey
Clifford Queen, Newark, Delaware
Marsha Rice, Winchester, Massachusetts
Dale Richmond, Augusta, Maine
Fred Smith, E. Weymouth, Massachusetts, and his wife, Monique

In Canada, a new addition to the Board is Laverne Corbett of Rothesay, New Brunswick.

New Canadian chaplains include:
Phyllis Johnston, Rothesay, New Brunswick
Valarie Barker, Rothesay, New Brunswick
Kaye Clark, Rothesay, New Brunswick

Heather Keith, Rothesay, New Brunswick
Linda Crawford, Rothesay, New Brunswick

CCS-Canada is anticipating, in the immediate future and with warranted enthusiasm, the training of somewhere between eight and fifteen new chaplains at their headquarters in Rothesay, New Brunswick. Training will be done by their officially retired but forever tireless champion of his Faith, Earl Hodgkins, who, with his wife Joan, still takes the ferry from his outpost Island of White Head back to the Island of Grand Manan to spend one day a week at the nursing home there, weather permitting!

In the United States office, on December 31, 1996, Executive Director Walter Dryer followed through with his plans to retire from the directorship and to return to the chaplain ministry. The Board of Directors appointed the Reverend David V. Schaffer to the position of Executive Director as of January 1, 1997.

Reverend Schaffer, a graduate of Boston University School of Theology and Bethel College, pastored several churches prior to his coming to CCS. He has served as a chaplain *par excellence* in seven nursing homes in southern Massachusetts and Rhode Island for nearly ten years and will be sorely missed in that role for which he is so significantly gifted. He is wished God's great wisdom and direction as he functions in this administrative role.

The part-time secretary's hours have been increased to sixteen a week, and a new computer system has been purchased and is in place. Chaplains' training has been increased to two weeks.

Seminars continue to be an inspirational and informative interlude for the chaplains each fall. Subjects covered the first two years of this third decade are:
1995 Understanding Dementia
1996 The Pursuit of Holiness

ECFA (Evangelical Council for Financial Accountability) certification has been consistently maintained.

A large gift of stock, graciously given for two years, has provided a much- needed boost to the financial burden of chaplain support. Income for 1996 totaled $204,000, which breaks down to $3900+ weekly—the highest in CCS history. However, the continual recruitment of chaplains will be dependent upon the funds made available by increasing numbers who see the need and who care.

According to the most recent figures available, the projected total United States population by the year 2050 is expected to reach 380 million. At least 7 percent, or some twenty-six million elderly, will probably be nursing home residents, compared with the 1.75 million now in residence. Nursing homes obviously are here to stay and opportunities will be limitless.

Our chaplains made over 84,000 visits last year alone and yet these represent a small fraction of the human beings who have had to leave home, family, and everything familiar; handle their grief and many times their anger; and try to adjust, or else just simply give up. They must not be allowed to feel that they are part of the typical throw-away mentality. Those who are sitting and waiting for someone to come to see them, just for themselves, need to hear that they are still important to someone, and most of all important to God!

As we look back over the past two decades, we see no explanation for the existence of CCS except that God was the Architect and Builder of a ministry which, due to His omniscience He foresaw, due to His omnipotence He crafted, and due to His omnipresence He oversees. With these attributes ever in place, the future can be as bright as are all of His purposes.

EPILOGUE

Since the writing of this story I have reflected again and again as to my real purpose in sharing with others these events in our lives. In so doing, I found a need to reevaluate, and the order of things assumed a reverse position as to their importance.

Increasingly I have asked myself, "Is the purpose here to glory in CCS, in Dave's being used to start something that will outlive him, something that has already been and should continue to be of enormous benefit to many?" As I ask myself this question I keep hearing in my head the Brooklyn Tabernacle Choir singing with their marvelous enthusiasm and conviction, "His Name Be Glorified!"

Therefore, my main purpose must be to send this message: That He desires, first of all, for us to find out who He really is and what He desires to be to us; that when we will permit Him to do so, God will function as a Father and Provider in ways we cannot even imagine; and that as we allow Him to show us about Himself, we may at the same time find Him showing us what we can do for Him. These are humbling thoughts.

All else, including the founding of a very worthy organization, pales before the experience of finding God to be a truly personal God who can indeed be trusted with one's life. This, then, is the major purpose of the book. Strange that it took so long for me to get priorities straight!

This having been said, Dave and I find ourselves again in a place of trusting the same God with Dave's slow and, at times, agonizing journey through Alzheimer's.

What of the future? What of tomorrow? Who cleans the gutters? Who fixes the grill when the burner rusts out? Does God care about things like that? Yes He does, and He continues to provide His *special angels* for us as He did through our journey into trust.

Who provides the wisdom and patience when communication with a life-time partner becomes less and less possible? Who fills the void when companionship becomes disconnected? Is God really there by the fireside at bedtime, when I sit by myself with the kitty in my lap, and sense the need to share my stockpile of thoughts?

Yes, He is there as He has been all along, and my heart is made quiet at the end of perhaps not an easy day. All is well because He is our Friend, He knows we are here, and that is forever sufficient.

Appendix
CHRONOLOGY OF DATES AND MAJOR EVENTS

June 1973	Beginning of journey into CCS.
November 1973	Concept of one-on-one ministry.
April 1974	Actual organization of CCS.
	Statement of Faith, Articles of Incorporation, Constitution and By-Laws written.
	Deputation for financial base begun.
May 1974	First convert.
May – Dec 1974	Full time service to four homes. Average receipts $172 per week.
May 1975	Incorporation accomplished.
Dec 1974 – 1975	Deputation the major thrust with supporters in ten states.
	Volunteers used widely in visitation.
	Average receipts $241 per week.
April 1976	Glenn Havumaki became part-time chaplain.
October 1976	Glenn Havumaki became full-time chaplain.
1975 – 1984	Full seven-member Board chosen.
1981	Walt Dryer became chaplain.
1983	Walt Dryer became Associate Director.
1984	Two new chaplains added.
	Full time service to thirteen homes in three States.
	211 regular contributors.
	Average receipts $983 weekly.
1985 – 1994	Eleven additions and replacements to Board.

1986 Resignation of David Kimball, executive director.

Appointment of Walt Dryer, executive director.

Seven chaplains added.

Associate chaplain category added.

Fourteen associate chaplains added.

ECFA (Evangelical Council for Financial Accountability) certification established.

1989 Annual Fall seminars begun.

1991 CCS-Canada begun.

Average receipts $3396 weekly.

Thirty chaplains now serving in eleven States

74,000 personal visits, 330 services, and 130 decisions for Christ.

50 percent growth in chaplain staff.

1993 CCS-Canada fully established with five chaplains serving.

1995 Three new Board members added.

Seven chaplains added, making a total of thirty-two in the United States and six in Canada. Of the thirty-two, Marsha Rice is the first handicapped chaplain to serve.

1996 New computer system in place.

CCS-Canada chaplains assisted by four college students for three summer months under a Federal Education Grant called 'Advanced Education Jet Program.'

Nine chaplains now in Canada.

Resignation of executive director Walt Dryer honored with regrets, effective January 1st, 1997.

Average receipts $3923 weekly.

Continued search for new executive director.

1997 Chaplain David Schaffer begins duties as executive director.

As of January, twenty-six chaplains and associate chaplains now serve in the United States, and seven in Canada, adjustments in numbers reflecting retirements and other factors.

Addendum 1 - 1998
OUR CHAPLAINS
UNITED STATES

BRIAN AROLD, associate chaplain, is pastor-trained and while waiting with his wife and three small children for God's further direction, Brian works in a foundry, at a diary farm, and finds time for two nursing home services twice weekly in New York.

HELEN BERRY arrived in Taiwan under Conservative Baptists International in 1954, serving there until retirement in 1989. Upon being introduced to CCS by another chaplain in 1990 she is in her sixth year of service as an associate chaplain in Florida.

BILL CAIN came to the chaplain ministry after nearly thirty years of service with Nynex Corp. His weekly visits to his nursing home friends in North Middleboro, Massachusetts, as an associate chaplain are coupled with his retirement duties as a business consultant.

DOROTHY CHASE, widow of a pastor and a pastor in her own right, now retired, is a professional bridal-shop seamstress and enjoys one day each week as an associate chaplain with twenty to twenty-five residents in a nursing home in Taunton, Massachusetts.

BOB COLLINS, associate chaplain, holds a degree in Law and is employed by an Insurance Company in the field of Fidelity and Surety Bond Claims. He serves at a local nursing home twice weekly, both in one-on-one and group ministry.

ELSIE M. CORDIS, Physical Therapist and former laboratory assistant instructor, became an associate chaplain in 1988. She visits, one-on-one, in a 145 bed nursing home in Connecticut, serving both the physical and the spiritual needs of residents.

IVAN CROSSMAN demonstrated his heart for the elderly by holding weekly Bible studies in nursing homes, along with his thirty-six years of pastoral ministry. Now four years into retirement, he serves four homes full time in the Shelbourne Falls, Massachusetts, area.

TED DURGIN was a high school band director in Rhode Island, who became a chaplain upon his retirement from teaching in 1989. He and his wife, **JUNE**, shared in this new ministry until his homegoing, at which time she continued as an associate chaplain in Massachusetts.

CHRISTINE A. FERGUSON, an x-ray technician by vocation for thirty years, has been an associate chaplain since 1994 after many years of interest in nursing home residents. She attends Conservative Baptist Seminary of the East, Worcester, Massachusetts.

KAY FRIES, now retired, and prior to her service as a chaplain for CCS in Lititz, Pennsylvania, had been a missionary to the Philippines with her husband for twenty-eight years, returning and serving there alone courageously for two years following his death.

MELVILLE HATCHER, after serving the Lord in Argentina from 1951-1986 for Conservative Baptists International, entered the Chaplain ministry in Florida where he visits four homes weekly with a variety of very effective personal and group techniques.

LEE HAUSE and his wife, **ARLENE**, after twenty-nine years as church planters in Chile, South America, and five years with the Gospel Mission of South America in Florida, are now in their sixth year of service as associate chaplains to four nursing homes in Pennsylvania.

JEAN JANUARY, wife of Coast-guardsman Jarrod, looks forward to an associate ministry on Cape Cod, Massachusetts, stimulated by working with seniors in her church and by meeting those who had needs in their lives. She is presently involved in more training.

WILLIAM KELLEY wears several hats, including musician, clinical psychologist, co-Pastor, and associate chaplain. He is in touch with eleven nursing homes in his state of New Jersey and rejoices in seven decisions for Christ during the past year.

LLOYDE LOWE and his wife, **MILLIE**, were appointed to CCS in 1983 after having served Conservative Baptists International in Brazil since 1951. They have served thirteen years in Massachusetts and Florida until their formal retirement in 1996.

ADELE OFFRINGA came to CCS as an associate chaplain after losing her husband to Heaven. She joined **JUNE DURGIN** where the two widows visit bed-to-bed, and share a hymn sing twice a month for some thirty-five residents and staff in a home in Wareham, Massachusetts.

CLIFF OLSON, former airforce jet mechanic who found the Lord in Korea during World War II, has served as chaplain for five years after thirty years in the ministry. He visits six homes weekly in the area of Jay, Maine, assisted by his wife, **WILMA**.

BILL PAIGE came to the chaplain service in 1986 after many years of pastor/associate pastor duties in and around New Hampshire, upon realizing that his special skills lay in serving nursing home residents. He now serves 850 residents in six homes weekly.

HARVEY PIERCE, a pastor of forty years experience, is a graduate of Asbury College in Kentucky. He heard of CCS through Director Walt and shares his retirement years as an associate chaplain in a nursing home ministry with his wife, **LORRAINE**, in Marion, Massachusetts.

CLIFFORD QUEEN is an octogenarian, and a former Marine who saw service in Guadalcanal. He is retired officially but serves as an associate chaplain on a regular basis at nursing homes and uses his deafness as an asset with those similarly afflicted!

DARWIN RANSOM pastors a church in Corinth, Vermont, full-time while carrying on his long-time sewing machine repair business. Although not officially a chaplain at the present time, he and his wife Joan still carry on a weekly nursing home ministry.

MARSHA RICE is a forty-six-year-old handicapped grandmom, and a graduate of Andover-Newton Theological Seminary who holds degrees in several other fields. She raises two special-needs grandchildren and visits four nursing homes in Massachusetts as associate chaplain.

DALE RICHMOND is a disabled veteran who naturally has a special sensitivity toward the veteran population. He visits as an associate chaplain in two areas twice weekly, one of which is the Maine Veteran's Home in Augusta, Maine.

TOM RYDER was a tractor-trailer driver and part-time chaplain during 1992 who was left totally disabled due to an accident in 1993. He is now serving God as an associate chaplain in three nursing homes in the area of Chadds Ford, Pennsylvania.

DAVID V. SCHAFFER in his earlier years served as pastor of several churches during which time he became a Christian! He and his wife, **RUTH**, started their chaplain ministry in 1987, and serve seven homes in southeastern Massachusetts and Rhode Island.

FRED SMITH, a semi-retired Interior Decorator, spends two or three days weekly at a nursing home in Massachusetts. He plans a monthly worship service with assistance from his church, and pursues a one-on-one associate ministry with his wife, **MONIQUE**.

ALAN T. SUTTON, a pastor with a heart for people, was appointed a chaplain in 1996. He is enjoying an exciting relationship with new friends, both staff and residents, in his nursing home areas in Rhode Island.

STEPHEN WOODWARD is a retired businessman who does a variety of nursing home ministries as an associate chaplain in Connecticut. Details unfortunately are not immediately available.

CCS Canada

VALARIE BARKER, a graduate of Atlantic Baptist College, is a member of Rothesay Baptist Church and is actively involved in a nursing home ministry because of a love for the elderly and because she found them to be neglected and needy.

KAYE CLARK has always loved the elderly and became aware of the CCS ministry at Rothesay Baptist Church. Because of a particular burden for Alzheimer's patients, she trained for and now visits that ward at Loch Lomond Villa each week.

LINDA CRAWFORD learned of the great nursing home needs through her daughter, Carla, who was a summer student chaplain. Her heart was touched at a presentation by Canadian Chairman Ken Anthony, and she now works as a team with Phyllis Johnston.

PHYLLIS JOHNSTON assisted her husband, **TERRY**, by playing and singing but was never comfortable visiting residents. One night while listening to his presentation of his ministry at a Missions Conference her heart was touched. She is now a chaplain.

TERRY JOHNSTON started his ministry by visiting one day a week; he soon enlarged his ministry to three or four days a week, and became acting Canadian Director. He recruits new chaplains, presents the ministry to churches, and encourages other chaplains.

HEATHER KEITH, now a chaplain, had negative feelings about the elderly due to poor childhood experiences. God used one positive experience to turn her heart around; she learned of the need in nursing homes and contacted Terry Johnston. The rest is history!

STEWART MOEN was told by one of his professors at Acadia Divinity College that he was suited to a seniors ministry. After his graduation, he learned of CCS and since that time has ministered at the Fairview Villa in Halifax, Nova Scotia.

Addendum 2 - 2010

An update on CCS since this book was first written finds us with Rev. William Echols as Executive Director since January 1, 2004, with 65 chaplains in this country, and 4 in the Philippines.

The Canadian chapter with Executive Director Robert Wadell has 18 chaplains ministering in areas ranging from Nova Scotia and New Brunswick to British Columbia.

Last year, 2008, our Chaplains made over 106 thousand one-on-one calls to nursing home residents. Our desire and prayer is that we will continue to grow nationally and internationally, and that the number of those who find faith in Christ will also grow.

Our Board's goal at this time, among its other goals, is working to establish a strong financial base to better support those who so eagerly give of themselves to serve these nearly forgotten elderly.

Statistics say that one third of them have only 2 visitors a year! We desire to change their 'warehouse' existence to one of feeling their personal worth once again, and of knowing the God who loves them.

ABOUT THE AUTHOR

Told repeatedly by others her story was too compelling to go unwritten, Gwen Bibber Kimball penned *You Say WHAT, Lord?: A Journey into Trust*, a book which reflects both her and her husband's belief and trust in God.

A native of Eastport, Maine, and now retired, Kimball and her husband of fifty–six years, David, live in New Bedford, Massachusetts. She is an active member of Mullein Hill Church, Lakeville, Massachusetts, which she calls "a busy involved place." Kimball also enjoys people, gardening, sailing, antiques, and music.

Gwen Bibber Kimball is available for speaking engagements and personal appearances. For more information contact:

Gwen Bibber Kimball
C/O Advantage Books
P.O. Box 160847
Altamonte Springs, Florida 32716

To purchase additional copies of this book or other books published by Advantage Books call our toll free order number at:
1-888-383-3110 (Book Orders Only)

or visit our bookstore website at:
www.advbookstore.com

Longwood, Florida, USA
"we bring dreams to life"™
www.advbooks.com

www.ingramcontent.com/pod-product-compliance
Lightning Source LLC
Chambersburg PA
CBHW020020050426
42450CB00005B/561